T0339460

Futurize! Dealing with Megatrends and Disruptors

The future will bring only more megatrends and disruptions. With the guidance of this book, which centers around the authors' years-of-research-backed high-performance organizations (HPO) framework and includes the unique self-assessment tool Futurize! diagnosis, business leaders and organizations will be prepared and truly future-ready.

The next two decades will present massive challenges for organizations, as they navigate the need for sustainable development against a complex backdrop of factors such as increasing inequality, resource scarcity, continued globalization, and the ever-increasing speed of technological advancement. This book will help business leaders and organizations set priorities and make decisions so that not only do they honor commitments to the United Nations Sustainable Development Goals, but also become more future-ready by:

- identifying the megatrends and disruptors which impact organizations now and will in the future
- specifically outlining how those megatrends and disruptors will impact organizations
- showing how organizations can deal with this impact in practical terms.

This book is a must for management teams, aspiring leaders, and professionals and students interested in the future of work, human resource management, and innovation.

André de Waal is Academic Director of the HPO Center and a partner at the Finance Function Research and Development Center, the Netherlands. He has been a consultant and past partner with Arthur Andersen for 16 years and served as Associate Professor of Organizational Effectiveness at the Maastricht School of Management for 13 years. Previously André lectured at the Free University Amsterdam, University of Amsterdam, and Erasmus University Rotterdam. He holds an MSc in chemistry from Leiden University, the Netherlands; an MBA from Northeastern University Boston, USA; and a PhD in economics from Vrije Universiteit Amsterdam, the Netherlands. He has published more than 400 articles and 36 books on high performance and performance management.

Julie Linthorst is an entrepreneur, researcher, and management consultant who specializes in the areas of organization design, sustainable human resources management, and the future of work. She holds an MSc in work and organization psychology from the University of Amsterdam and a BSc degree in small business management from Hogeschool Inholland. After having worked at globally recognized consultancy firms and with Arthur Andersen as Senior Manager for developing human capital, Julie started her own firm in 2002. She has since worked as a consultant for large multinationals, SMEs, and government agencies. Julie volunteers to support poverty alleviation and social inclusion. Her research has been published in multiple peer-reviewed journals, and she has spoken at several notable scientific conferences, such as the European Academy of Management (EURAM) and the British Academy of Management (BAM). Julie is currently undertaking a PhD in the future of work at Nyenrode Business Universiteit, the Netherlands.

Futurize! Dealing with Megatrends and Disruptors

A Handbook for the Future-Oriented CEO

André de Waal and Julie Linthorst

Routledge
Taylor & Francis Group

NEW YORK AND LONDON

Cover image: Andre Klijsen

First published in English 2022
by Routledge
605 Third Avenue, New York, NY 10158

and by Routledge
4 Park Square, Milton Park, Abingdon, Oxon, OX14 4RN

Routledge is an imprint of the Taylor & Francis Group, an informa business

Published in Dutch by Van Duuren Management 2021

Library of Congress Cataloging-in-Publication Data
Names: Waal, André de, author. | Linthorst, Julie, author.
Title: Futurize! Dealing with megatrends and disruptors :
    a handbook for the future-oriented CEO / André de Waal
    and Julie Linthorst.
Description: New York, NY : Routledge, 2022. | Includes
    bibliographical references and index.
Identifiers: LCCN 2021059346 | ISBN 9781032226064
    (hardback) | ISBN 9781032226057 (paperback) |
    ISBN 9781003273264 (ebook)
Subjects: LCSH: Organizational effectiveness. | Strategic
    planning. | Industrial management.
Classification: LCC HD58.9 .W329 2022 | DDC
    658.4/012—dc23/eng/20220504
LC record available at https://lccn.loc.gov/2021059346

ISBN: 978-1-032-22606-4 (hbk)
ISBN: 978-1-032-22605-7 (pbk)
ISBN: 978-1-003-27326-4 (ebk)

DOI: 10.4324/9781003273264

Typeset in Sabon
by Apex CoVantage, LLC

Contents

About the authors

Dr. André de Waal, MSc, MBA, PhD, is Managing Partner and Academic Director of the HPO Center, an organization that conducts research into high-performance organizations. He is also a partner at the Finance Function Research and Development Center, a company that aims to help finance functions to transform in a high-performing department. André has been a consultant and partner with Arthur Andersen for 16 years. André was also Associate Professor of Organizational Effectiveness for 13 years at the Maastricht School of Management. He has been a guest lecturer at the Free University Amsterdam, University of Amsterdam, and Erasmus University Rotterdam; a visiting fellow at Cranfield University, UK; and a senior lecturer at Wittenborg University of Applied Sciences. André holds an MSc in chemistry from Leiden University, the Netherlands; an MBA from Northeastern University Boston, USA; and a PhD in economics from Vrije Universiteit Amsterdam, the Netherlands. His dissertation was about the behavioral aspects that are important for the successful implementation and use of performance management systems.

André teaches and does projects in the field of high-performance organizations and performance management in many countries, such as Australia, China, Vietnam, Bangladesh, Mongolia, Nepal, Mexico, Peru, Ecuador, Suriname, the United States, the United Kingdom, Italy, Belgium, Portugal, Poland, Saudi Arabia, Yemen, the United Arab Emirates, Palestine, South Africa, Namibia, Tanzania, and Zambia. He was selected by managementboek.nl as one of the Dutch Masters in Management, ten people who have influenced management thinking in the Netherlands the most in the past decade.

André has published more than 400 articles (among which are more than 130 academic publications) and 35 books on organizational improvement and performance management. Among his English books are *Power of Performance Management, How Leading Companies Create Sustained Value* (John Wiley & Sons, 2001), *Quest for Balance: The Human Element in Performance Management Systems*

(John Wiley & Sons, 2002), *What Makes a High-Performance Organization* (Global Professional Publishing, 2012), *Strategic Performance Management* (Palgrave MacMillan, second edition, 2013), and *High-Performance Managerial Leadership* (Praeger, 2020). His articles can be read on www.hpocenter.com and www.andredewaal.eu.

Websites:

www.hpocenter.com
www.ffrd.nl
www.andredewaal.eu

Julie Linthorst, MA, BSc, is a psychologist and business administrator. She has many years of knowledge and broad experience in the field of human resources management in many different sectors. As a daughter in an entrepreneurial family, she was taught flexibility, creativity, and a solution-oriented approach at an early age. Julie is known for seeing opportunities everywhere and taking advantage of them. It was, therefore, only logical that she would turn these qualities into her profession. Julie started her career as an associate researcher at the University of Amsterdam, after which she made the switch to the corporate world. There she worked as a consultant at PWC and subsequently at Arthur Andersen, where she was Senior Manager for developing and marketing human capital solutions. In 2001 she decided to start her own consultancy practice. She focuses on organizational design, performance management, and human resources management. Because of her pragmatic approach, Julie is often asked to sit on trust and objection committees.

In addition to her consultancy practice, Julie has started various initiatives, such as organizing training camps for elite sports teams in Spain and www.kickboxclinics.nl. The latter organization focuses on improving resilience in teams through kickboxing clinics. All experiences— successful or less successful—have influenced her growth as an entrepreneur and adviser. Julie knows better than anyone what it is like to create your own job, to work as a flex (flexible) worker, to deal with uncertainty, and to ensure that you remain permanently employable. During her period as an independent entrepreneur, she has followed various courses. In 2020, for example, she completed the intervention studies course at the Academy of Intervention Studies. Her advice is to always keep learning, even if you have a family next to your work and need to keep many balls in the air simultaneously.

Julie is committed to social issues, such as sustainable employability and combating poverty and inequality. Her vision is that in an inclusive world, everyone can benefit. Since 2020 she has been doing her PhD research at Nyenrode Business University, focused on the future of work. Her interest lies in the way in which organizations prepare for the future and what meaningful actions they can take. With her PhD research, she wants to bundle, test, and share all her knowledge within a future of work research community, making use of collective intelligence and AI tooling. She expects to be able to contribute to how you can actively and confidently face the future. To date, the research has resulted in multiple publications in peer-reviewed journals, and she has spoken at scientific conferences such as the European Academy of Management (EURAM) and the British Academy of Management (BAM). Julie enjoys working with students and young people. She regularly gives guest lectures in which the contents of this book are discussed.

Websites:

www.julielinthorst.com
www.wefuturize.com
www.kickboxclinics.nl

Prologue

A wake-up call

In August 2019, we received an email from a large multinational inquiring into our availability to conduct a high-performance organization (HPO) workshop with their top management during the yearly retreat called Strategy Days. These types of emails are not uncommon for us, and we happily agreed to this invitation.

However, the original date in December was not convenient for us because of prior client commitments, and after some deliberation, the meeting was postponed to March 2020 and moved from Geneva to Wuhan. Now, we admit freely that at that time, we were not familiar with this city; we had to look it up on Wikipedia. It turned out to be a metropolis in Central Eastern China, with ten million inhabitants, forming an interchange connecting North and South China as well as East and West China via railways, highways, and the Yangtze River. Carefree, we at that time thought it would be nice to visit this new place.

But as often happens with something or someone you had never heard of before, suddenly you start to hear and read all kinds of things about it or them. And what we heard in the month of December about Wuhan was quite alarming—rumors and stories about a new virus that was creating havoc in the city. The stories grew in number, so much so that in January 2020, we sent an email to our contact person at the client asking what was going on and whether the meeting would continue as planned.

By return mail, we got the answer: "DO NOT BOOK YOUR FLIGHT YET, WE'LL GET BACK TO YOU." Needless to say, the meeting was again rescheduled, both in time and place, to eventually be canceled completely. COVID-19, caused by the virus SARS-CoV-2, had not only hit Wuhan but had by that time taken the whole world by surprise. A true wake-up call for humanity!

Book content

This book comprises 18 chapters aimed at, first, introducing the megatrends and disruptors that can and will affect the future of work in organizations; second, introducing the high-performance organization (HPO) framework, which gives direction to the way organizations can and should respond to the megatrends and disruptors; and third, introducing the Futurize! process with which organizations can evaluate their future-readiness and develop actions to make them better prepared for a future of megatrends and disruptors.

The book is organized as follows:

Chapter 1: Purpose of this book
COVID-19 has had a big impact on society and organizations. The way both reacted to this pandemic, which was not the first disruptor the world encountered and certainly will not be the last, left something to be desired. The emerging "new normal" forces organizations to adapt their business operations to fit the new situation, which comes on top of the current megatrends or disruptors. This chapter defines these megatrends and disruptors, provides a reading guide for the book, and discusses the added value of the book.

Chapter 2: Identification of the megatrends and disruptors
First, a distinction has to be clearly made between megatrends and disruptors. There is a difference between changes that gradually take place over a longer period of time (i.e., the *megatrends*) and short-term, seemingly unexpected sharp changes with high impact (i.e., the *disruptors*). In this chapter, the research into the identification of the thirteen megatrends and one disruptor that already are or will be exerting much influence on the business operations of organizations now or in the near future is described.

Chapter 3: The high-performance organization framework
To discover and develop courses of action to address the identified megatrends and disruptor, the HPO (high-performance organization) framework has been used. An HPO—defined as an organization

that achieves financial and non-financial results that outperform its peers/competitors over a period of five years or more by focusing in a disciplined manner on what is truly important to the organization— is seen as an organization that can thrive through disruption as they are known for their flexibility and adaptability, which enable them to cope well with changing circumstances. In this chapter, the HPO framework is described, and the practices that will help HPOs better prepare for the future are developed. These practices will then be useful to other organizations, regardless of their current performance level.

Chapter 4: Speed of technological advancement: Megatrend 1

This chapter deals with technological advancement, which is the collective name for the increasing speed of change in the field of technological and digital tools that increase productivity and provide better access to information and ideas. It is the increasing speed of change in technology that makes technological progress a force for change. In the chapter, the expected effects of this megatrend on organizations and the future of work are described, in terms of both opportunities and threats, its relation to the other megatrends and the disruptor, and how an organization can evaluate its preparedness to deal with the speed of technological advancement.

Chapter 5: Flexible employment: Megatrend 2

This chapter deals with increasing flexible employment, which refers to the growing variation in work arrangements and practices. It is expected that traditional nine-to-five jobs will change to remote and on-demand work, as mobile technology and the Internet no longer require employees to work in the same fixed location. There will also be an increase in "liquid" positions and jobs, in which people have multiple roles within one organization or work as independent contractors for multiple organizations at the same time. In the chapter, the expected effects of this megatrend on organizations and the future of work are described, in terms of both opportunities and threats, its relation to the other megatrends and the disruptor, and how an organization can evaluate its preparedness to deal with flexible employment.

Chapter 6: Skills mismatch: Megatrend 3

This chapter deals with the increasing gaps between the skills the current workforce has and the skills needed for the jobs of the future. With the increasing speed of change, it is seen as a challenge to prepare organizations, employees, and educational systems in a timely manner for the changing workplace. Moreover, it is not yet entirely clear what these changes to the workplace precisely entail and what new skills are exactly required. In the chapter, the expected effects of this megatrend on organizations and the future of work are described, in terms of both opportunities and threats, its relation to the other megatrends and the disruptor, and how an organization can evaluate its preparedness to deal with the skills mismatch.

Chapter 7: Sustainable employment: Megatrend 4

This chapter deals with an increasing demand for and need for sustainable employment, which refers to the extent to which employees want and can continue to work now and in the future at an organization. It is about providing work and working conditions that keep employees happy, healthy, and motivated. There is a growing concern for this because of the impending workforce shortage due to the aging workforce, coupled with a growing awareness of sustainability in general among the population and, therefore, among the organization's customers. In the chapter, the expected effects of this megatrend on organizations and the future of work are described, in terms of both opportunities and threats, its relation to the other megatrends and the disruptor, and how an organization can evaluate its preparedness to deal with sustainable employment.

Chapter 8: Continued globalization: Megatrend 5

This chapter deals with continuing globalization, which is the process by which companies and other organizations develop more international influence or (start to) operate in an international environment. An alternative interpretation of globalization is the growing interaction and integration between people, companies, and governments worldwide. The phenomenon is not new but is expected to continue in the near future. In light of the COVID-19 pandemic, which caused global problems in manufacturing and logistics, there was a slightly emerging trend of deglobalization in the field of crucial products. However, it is still unclear whether this movement will continue. In the chapter, the expected effects of this megatrend on organizations and the future of work are described, in terms of both opportunities and threats, its relation to the other megatrends and the disruptor, and how an organization can evaluate its preparedness to deal with continuing globalization.

Chapter 9: Changing workforce composition: Megatrend 6

This chapter deals with the changing composition of the workforce, which was set in motion by an aging population and shifts in generations working in an organization. Older employees are a growing part of the workplace, and they work longer. At the same time, the generational shift results in major changes in the composition of the workforce. By 2025, millennials will make up the largest part of the workforce. In the chapter, the expected effects of this megatrend on organizations and the future of work are described, in terms of both opportunities and threats, its relation to the other megatrends and the disruptor, and how an organization can evaluate its preparedness to deal with the changing composition of its workforce.

Chapter 10: Increasing inequality: Megatrend 7

This chapter deals with increasing inequality in the world that has an effect on the business world. There is growing concern about rising wage and income inequality. While overall (pre-corona) employment rates have risen globally, several groups of workers have not benefited equally, and their situation is deteriorating—especially low-skilled workers, workers with jobs that are in danger of disappearing due to automation, self-employed persons/gig workers, and workers with a migration background are at risk. In addition, the gender gap (which also leads to wage differences between employees) is not expected to disappear anytime soon. In the chapter, the expected effects of this megatrend on organizations and the future of work are described, in terms of both opportunities and threats, its relation to the other megatrends and the disruptor, and how an organization can evaluate its preparedness to deal with the increasing inequality.

Chapter 11: Environmental issues: Megatrend 8

This chapter deals with the changes in the global climate caused by human activity and their consequences. Floods, sea-level rise, forest fires, extreme weather events, and natural disasters lead to major disruptions to everyday (business) life. Climate change is expected to have a huge negative impact on future economic growth, as significant investments are needed to reduce the ecological footprint of people and businesses, promote sustainability and protect the environment, and deal with the expected migration of people from countries with the greatest environmental issues. In the chapter, the expected effects of this megatrend on organizations and the future of work are described, in terms of both opportunities and threats, its relation to the other megatrends and the disruptor, and how an organization can evaluate its preparedness to deal with environmental issues.

Chapter 12: Economic power shifts: Megatrend 9

This chapter deals with the shift of economic power from the traditional West to the emerging East. Countries in this region are becoming economically bigger and more important due to an increase in their middle class. The emerging markets will rewrite the rules of work and work culture as a result of their economic growth, and their political power will increase. This will have and, in fact, already has an impact on the competitive position of organizations in Western countries. In the chapter, the expected effects of this megatrend on organizations and the future of work are described, in terms of both opportunities and threats, its relation to the other megatrends and the disruptor, and how an organization can evaluate its preparedness to deal with the economic power shifts.

Chapter 13: Urbanization: Megatrend 10

This chapter deals with the global migration of people from rural to urban areas, resulting in an increasing number of people becoming permanently concentrated in relatively small areas (cities or metropolitan areas). This has implications for organizations: in rural areas, there can be a shortage of qualified workers, while urban areas become too crowded. The first leads to organizational problems; the second, to higher living costs, competition for jobs, and a more hectic/unbalanced life and, consequently, health problems. In the chapter, the expected effects of this megatrend on organizations and the future of work are described, in terms of both opportunities and threats, its relation to the other megatrends and the disruptor, and how an organization can evaluate its preparedness to deal with increasing urbanization.

Chapter 14: Cross-border migration: Megatrend 11

This chapter deals with the migration of workers from their home countries to other countries with the aim of finding (better) work. Cross-border migration is a consequence of a world in which people do not find attractive employment opportunities in their country of origin, at a time when other economies cannot adequately fill their labor shortages. This migration changes the composition of the workforce and can lead to social problems. In the chapter, the expected effects of this megatrend on organizations and the future of work are described, in terms of both opportunities and threats, its relation to the other megatrends and the disruptor, and how an organization can evaluate its preparedness to deal with growing cross-border migration.

Chapter 15: Resource scarcity: Megatrend 12

This chapter deals with the ever-increasing global demand for resources (such as water, food, energy, land, and minerals), which causes scarcity and inherent increases in costs. Organizations increasingly need to rethink and tackle their dependence on scarce raw materials and resources by finding new ways of working, innovating, and using alternative means and techniques. In addition, society and customers will force organizations to minimize their negative impact on society and the environment. In the chapter, the expected effects of this megatrend on organizations and the future of work are described, in terms of both opportunities and threats, its relation to the other megatrends and the disruptor, and how an organization can evaluate its preparedness to deal with resource scarcities.

Chapter 16: Individualism: Megatrend 13

This chapter deals with the trend among people to distinguish oneself from another as a person, as an individual. This trend is a result of a shift from a collectivist society to a greater focus on the individual and society's increasing expectations about the availability of goods and services at any time and in the shape and form one desires. Thus, people and organizations increasingly expect tailor-made and personalized products, services, and solutions. In the chapter, the expected effects of this megatrend on organizations and the future of work are described, in terms of both opportunities and threats, its relation to the other megatrends and the disruptor, and how an organization can evaluate its preparedness to deal with increasing individualism.

Chapter 17: Pandemics: Disruptor 1

This chapter deals with pandemics, which place extraordinary demands on public health and medical care and threaten the functioning and even survival of organizations. Major outbreaks have serious, often long-lasting consequences for individuals, businesses, and society as a whole. The ensuing economic and fiscal effects often last longer than the epidemiological consequences themselves. In the chapter, the expected effects of this megatrend on organizations and the future of work are described, in terms of both opportunities and threats, its relation to the other megatrends and the disruptor, and how an organization can evaluate its preparedness to deal with future pandemics.

Chapter 18: The Futurize! process

This chapter brings the preceding chapters on megatrends and disruptors together by offering a practical way in which an organization can evaluate and prepare itself for the future. In the so-called Futurize! process, the organization maps out the megatrend or disruptor that is expected to have an impact and determines the extent to which it is prepared for the megatrend or disruptor. During this process, the Futurize! diagnosis is used, which consists of a self-assessment that is filled in and subsequently discussed by the members of the management team and other knowledgeable people in the organization. The result of the Futurize! diagnosis is a commonly supported view of the organization's readiness for the future and what needs to be done to make it future-ready.

Chapter 1

Purpose of this book

In the pre-COVID-19 era, much management literature started with the observation that the rate of change was very high. Looking back now, we can say that that time was an oasis of calm and stability.[1]

1.1 The new normal

To state, at the time of writing this book (summer 2021), that the COVID-19 pandemic has had a great impact on society and the business community is clearly an understatement.[2]

According to the SHRM Association,[3] based on a survey of more than 2,000 HR professionals, one-third of the employers where these surveyed professionals worked had no emergency preparedness plans to deal with disasters. Of those who did have a plan, more than half did not include policies covering communicable diseases. Most employers were struggling to adapt to remote working and reported that they had difficulty maintaining morale among their employees, leading to over a third of them suffering from decreased productivity. This forced 40% of the organizations to shut down certain aspects of their business, with another 19% contemplating doing the same and 10% even facing a total shutdown. In total, 83% of the organizations had to adapt their business practices to the new situation (i.e., no more new hires, decreased hours and/or pay rates for employees, layoffs, offering paid or unpaid leave), with another 8% considering doing the same. Similar disturbing figures are reported by many other sources.[4] To make matters worse, organizations rarely allocate enough resources to prepare for, let alone deal with, crises such as pandemics.[5]

DOI: 10.4324/9781003273264-1

The situation created by the COVID-19 pandemic is already popularly called the "new normal," which is described as "a situation of radical change, consistent with a large exogenous shock experienced by firms and society at large. Such shock can be a radical change in institutions or a broader-environment-related shock. Through many cascading effects, somewhat like those found in ecological systems, the shock structurally changes behaviors."[6]

The new normal forces organizations to adapt their business operations to fit the new situation. It comes on top of the current disruptions organizations have to deal with in their environments. These disruptions can take the shape of megatrends or disruptors:

- *Megatrends* are described as large social, economic, political, and technological changes that are slow to form, but once in place, they have an influence for some time, between seven or ten years or longer.[7]
- A *disruptor* is defined as "someone or something that prevents something, especially a system, process or event, from continuing as usual or as expected."[8]

The main difference between megatrends and disruptors is the speed with which they appear and the effects they have—megatrends are changes that (often gradually) take place over a longer period of time, while disruptors are short-term, seemingly unexpected sharp changes with high impact.[9] Both can present business opportunities, but more often than not, they are seen as threats to future business growth or even to the sustainability of the organization.[10]

To illustrate our earlier remark that the COVID-19 pandemic took the world by surprise, we look at the research into megatrends and disruptors, which we started in the summer of 2019. At that time, we could only find megatrends in the academic literature on the "future of work," there was no mention of disruptors, such as a pandemic in relation to impact on and consequences for organizations at all! In this sense COVID-19 was a *wake-up call* for us. We had already noticed that academic literature was not that supportive in helping organizations deal with megatrends as there was hardly any advice or ways of copying discussed in that type of literature. Now we found that the same was true for disruptors like COVID-19 and that the managerial literature was no help either.

We needed to expand our scope and search fields to include additional literature that did discuss pandemics. We also came to the understanding that organizations desperately needed advice not only to help them deal with COVID-19 but also to prepare themselves for the occurrence of future disruptors and for dealing with current megatrends. Thus, we decided to expand our original two academic articles that documented the results of our research[11] into a managerial book aimed at providing organizations with information about the megatrends and disruptors that they need to deal with now and in the (near) future. But we go one step further than just providing information; we also discuss the courses of action with which organizations can prepare themselves for these megatrends and disruptors. These courses of action help organizations to decide how to adapt their business operations to fit new situations created by (rapidly) changing circumstances. In addition, we will present you with the Futurize! diagnosis, with which you can gauge how ready and prepared your organization is for a future riddled with megatrends and disruptors. The outcome of this self-assessment forms the start for the strategic foresight discussions you are going to conduct with people in your organization so that together you can make your organization future-ready. We wish you much success.

André de Waal & Julie Linthorst, September 2021

> A study on the impact of being forward-looking on organizational success found that so-called vigilant organizations that are consciously preparing for the future are 33 to 44% more profitable than those that do not. Vulnerable organizations with limited or almost no foresight practices have a 37% lower profitability. Companies that are struggling and have to fear for their survival because they do little about being forward-looking even have a 44% lower profitability.[12]

1.2 Reading guide

In Chapter 2, we describe the approach to our research with which we identified thirteen megatrends and one disruptor. This chapter first discusses the difference between a megatrend and a disruptor, after which the research method we used and the megatrends and the disruptor are discussed. In Chapter 3, we describe the HPO framework, which was the analysis tool during our research. Chapters 4 to 17 discuss the megatrends and the disruptor, one at a time. We provide a description of the megatrend/disruptor, describe its impact on organizations, discuss how it relates to the other megatrends and the disruptor, and how organizations can tackle the megatrend/disruptor. In *frames* scattered throughout the book, we give examples of ways in which the megatrend/disruptor manifests itself in practice and how organizations deal with it. These chapters can be read separately from each other, so they do not have to be read consecutively. In Chapter 18, we make our research results practical in the Futurize! process with, at its heart, the Futurize! diagnosis. In this chapter, we also give a number of practical examples of organizations that have used the Futurize! diagnosis.

Quick reading guide

As stated, not all chapters need to be read sequentially. We advise the reader in a hurry to read chapters 2, 3, and 18. With this, you are aware of the thirteen megatrends and the disruptor, the HPO framework, and the Futurize! diagnosis, which makes the results of our research (in which the megatrends and the disruptor are linked to the factors of the HPO framework) practically useful for your organization.

The practical value of this book is illustrated by this comment by Professor Lynda Gratton: "The future of work is one of the most burning platforms of the next few years. Time alone will tell whether the anguish will convert to action."[13] Our book helps organizational leaders with their decision-making and prioritization of improvement and innovation projects so that they adequately and effectively deal with their fears about the future of work—and thus the future of their organizations. As a result, they will not feel fear but will be proud of the resilience of their organization—and of their own resilience also because they have ensured the organizational sustainability of their organizations. Happy reading and good luck with Futurizing![14]

1.3 Acknowledgments

The cliché says that you never write a book alone. In our case, of course, that's completely appropriate because we wrote the book together. But even then, there is a group of people who have been invaluable in the production of this book, and we would like to thank them. First of all, many thanks to all the pilot organizations that participated in the development of the Futurize! process. In addition, there were people who contributed to the various roundtable discussions where parts of this book were discussed and fine-tuned. A number of people contributed beyond the call of duty: Gemma Cooymans, who did a lot of research, sorting out, and classification during the identification of the megatrends and disruptors; Caroline Hetterschijt, who contributed to two articles (which are incorporated in this book); and Monique Lindzen, who, as a publisher of Van Duuren Management, was immediately enthusiastic about the concept and published the Dutch version of the book. Finally, we are grateful to

Ken Lizotte for finding yet another great publishing home for our book. You all helped make this book future-proof—thank you for that!

Notes

1 Wagenaar (2020)
2 Hughes et al., 2020; Karabag, 2020; Kniffin et al., 2020; Shankar, 2020
3 SHRM Association, 2020
4 See, for instance, Beech and Anseel (2020), Eggers (2020), Kniffin et al. (2020), Koonin (2020), Wang et al. (2020).
5 Bowers et al., 2017; Burkle, 2010; McMenamin, 2009
6 Verbeke (2020, p. 444)
7 Naisbitt and Aburdene, 1990
8 Cambridge Dictionary, 2020
9 Waal and Linthorst, 2020
10 Bhalla et al., 2017; Cheung-Judge, 2017
11 Linthorst and Waal, 2020; Waal and Linthorst, 2020
12 Rohrbeck et al. (2018)
13 Gratton (2020a)
14 One might be wondering: isn't this book out of date at the time of going to press? After all, in a rapidly changing world, (mega) trends and disruptors follow each other in quick succession. Answer: no, the megatrends have been known for years; disruptors do change more rapidly. However, through the process of Futurize! you learn to look more ahead, to recognize (mega) trends and disruptors earlier, and to respond to those changes. Futurize! creates awareness.

Chapter 2

Identification of the megatrends and disruptors

In this chapter, we discuss our research into the identification of the megatrends and disruptors that already are or will be exerting much influence on the business operations of organizations now or in the near future.

2.1 The difference between megatrends and disruptors

We first make the distinction between megatrends and disruptors clear. There is a difference between changes that gradually take place over a longer period of time (i.e., the *megatrends*) and short-term, seemingly unexpected sharp changes with high impact (i.e., the *disruptors*).

Megatrends are larger in magnitude, longer in duration, and deeper in their effects than normal trends, fads, or fashions.[1] Naisbitt was the first to introduce the term *megatrends*, which he defined as socioeconomic or structural processes that are slowly forming but, once they occur, influence all areas of life for some time.[2] A few years later, he expanded the definition to "large social, economic, political, and technological changes that are slow to form, and once in place, have an influence for some time, between seven or ten years, or longer."[3] In subsequent years, many definitions were put forward in the literature of which many are a variation of Naisbitt's. Often the emphasis is put on the impact of a megatrend being extensive and global, in all areas of life and society and over a longer period of time.[4]

The Cambridge Dictionary describes a disruptor as "someone or something that prevents something, especially a system, process or event, from continuing as usual or as expected."[5] The National Intelligence Council states that disruptors (also called game changers or black swans) are, just as megatrends, transformational but that their occurrence and impact—where, when, the magnitude of effect—are uncertain and, therefore, difficult to plan for.[6] Thus, the main difference between megatrends and disruptors is the predictability of the occurrence and its impact or, in the

DOI: 10.4324/9781003273264-2

case of disruptors, their unpredictability. This distinction leads to differences in how organizations should deal with each of these changes

An occurrence last year showed how complex it could be to respond to a megatrend. Texas has invested a lot in green energy generation in recent decades. However, the extreme cold that year, combined with poor maintenance planning, created a serious energy crisis. Windmills froze, and because of the shutdown of oil refineries, the gas supply was also hindered. More than five million Americans were affected. This crisis raised the question of whether the energy transition to sustainable energy sources did not entail too many risks. However, according to experts, the underlying problem is poor maintenance planning and a lack of power connections to other US states.[7]

2.2 The research approach and results: thirteen megatrends and one disruptor

We identified the megatrends and the disruptor that will affect organizations in the (near) future during a search of the literature. We first searched various academic databases (EBSCO, Emerald, Google Scholar) using (a combination of) the keywords "megatrends," "disruptors," "future of work," and "4th Industrial Revolution." To be sure to focus on the latest insights so that the findings in these studies are relevant, we narrowed the scope of our search to the previous decade (2010–2020). We did not only look at the academic literature as it was rather scarce on the topic of megatrends and especially disruptors. We also examined the professional literature, using the same keywords, as the future of work and megatrends are prominent topics in various studies conducted by consultants and professional associations.

Based on the searches, we selected 162 relevant articles. These articles were searched for the following elements:

- Whether the article qualified as primary or secondary literature[8]
- What the scope of the article was in terms of industry, geography, and scientific discipline
- Whether the article had a monodisciplinary, multidisciplinary, or holistic view on the topic[9]
- Which megatrends or disruptors were given in the article
- What the (potential) impact of the megatrend or disruptor was expected to be on the future of work and organizations

We then grouped the megatrends and disruptors in categories of similarity (for example, "climate change" and "global warming" were clustered in the category "environmental issues"; "millennials," "generation Z," "crowded planet," and "demographic/aging" formed category "changing workforce composition") and counted the number of times the megatrends and/or disruptors in each category were mentioned in the selected articles. In this way, we arrived at a listing of the megatrends and the disruptor in order of frequency in which they were mentioned in the literature (see Table 2.1).

Table 2.1 The megatrends and the disruptor identified in the literature

Megatrend/ disruptor	Short description
Megatrend 1: Speed of technological advancement	Technological advancement is the collective name for the increasing speed of change in the field of technological and digital tools, such as automation, big data, and advanced analytics, that increase productivity and provide better access to information and ideas. Organizations have been automating work for decades, but it is the *increasing speed* of change in technology that makes technological progress a force for change.
Megatrend 2: Flexible employment	Flexible employment refers to the increasing variation in work arrangements and practices—for example, in a number of working hours/times, work locations (such as remote working/working from home), and types of employment contracts. It is expected that traditional nine-to-five jobs will change to remote and on-demand work, as mobile technology and the Internet no longer require employees to work in the same fixed location. There will also be an increase in "liquid" positions and jobs, in which people have multiple roles within one organization or work as independent contractors for multiple organizations at the same time. This is called the gig economy or network economy.
Megatrend 3: Skills mismatch	Skills mismatch refers to the expected skills gap between the skills the current workforce has and the skills needed for the jobs of the future. Learning new skills to adapt to the changing work environment is not a new phenomenon, but with the increasing speed of change, it is seen as a challenge to prepare organizations, employees, and

Megatrend/ disruptor	Short description
	educational systems in a timely manner for this changing workplace. Moreover, it is not yet entirely clear what these changes to the workplace precisely entail and what new skills are exactly required.
Megatrend 4: Sustainable employment	Sustainable employment (or similar concepts, such as sustainable work and decent work) refers to the extent to which employees want and can continue to work now and in the future. It is about providing work and working conditions that keep employees happy, healthy, and motivated. Managers have a growing awareness and concern for this because of the impending workforce shortage due to the aging workforce, coupled with a growing awareness of sustainability in general among the population and, therefore, among the organization's customers.
Megatrend 5: Continued globalization	Globalization is the process by which companies and other organizations develop more international influence or (start to) operate in an international environment. An alternative description of globalization is the growing interaction and integration between people, companies, and governments worldwide. The phenomenon is not new but is expected to continue in the near future. In light of the COVID-19 pandemic, which caused global problems in manufacturing and logistics, there was a slightly emerging trend of deglobalization. This mainly occurred in the field of crucial products, where countries wanted to produce these products internally. However, it is still unclear whether this movement will continue.
Megatrend 6: Changing workforce composition	The changing composition of the workforce is caused by an aging population and generational shifts. Older employees are not only a growing part of the workplace; they also work longer. Concerns about preserving benefits and income for healthcare and the desire to remain active and involved are some of the reasons older adults plan to work longer. At the same time, the generational shift results in major changes in the composition of the workforce. The baby boomer generation will be replaced by the millennials, followed by generation Z and generation A. By 2025, millennials will make up the largest part of the workforce.

(Continued)

Table 2.1 (Continued)

Megatrend/ disruptor	Short description
Megatrend 7: Increasing inequality	There is growing concern about rising wage and income inequality. While overall (pre-corona) employment rates have risen globally, there are several groups of workers who have not benefited equally, and their situation appears to be deteriorating—especially low-skilled workers, workers with jobs that are in danger of disappearing due to automation, self-employed persons/gig workers, and workers with a migration background are at risk. In addition, the gender gap (which also leads to wage differences between employees) is not expected to disappear anytime soon. Thus, there is an increasing need for social protection for vulnerable workers, with measures ranging from legal protection in flexible working arrangements to the introduction of a universal income.
Megatrend 8: Environmental issues	Environmental issues refer to changes in the global climate caused by human activity and their consequences. Floods, sea-level rise, forest fires, extreme weather events, and natural disasters caused by climate change lead to major disruptions to everyday life. Climate change is expected to have a huge negative impact on future economic growth, as significant investments are needed to reduce the ecological footprint of people and businesses, promote sustainability and protect the environment, and deal with the expected migration of people from countries with the greatest environmental issues.
Megatrend 9: Economic power shifts	Economic power shifts refer to the shift of economic power from the traditional West to the emerging East. Countries in Asia (and to a lesser extent South America and Africa) are becoming economically bigger and more important due to an increase in their middle class. The emerging markets will rewrite the rules of work and work culture as a result of their economic growth, and their political power will increase. This has an impact on the competitive position of organizations in Western countries: they become more vulnerable but at the same time get growth opportunities in the emerging regions.

Megatrend/ disruptor	Short description
Megatrend 10: Urbanization	Megatrend urbanization refers to the global migration of people from rural to urban areas, resulting in an increasing number of people becoming permanently concentrated in relatively small areas (cities or metropolitan areas). This has implications for organizations in both rural and urban areas. In rural areas, there can be a shortage of qualified workers, while urban areas become too crowded. The first leads to organizational problems; the second, to higher living costs, competition for jobs, and a more hectic/ unbalanced life and, consequently, health problems.
Megatrend 11: Cross-border migration	Cross-border migration refers to the migration of workers to other countries with the aim of finding (better) work. Cross-border migration is a natural consequence of a world in which people do not find attractive employment opportunities in their country of origin at a time when other economies cannot adequately fill their labor shortages. This migration changes the composition of the workforce and can lead to social problems. Moreover, migrant workers are more vulnerable than native workers and have a higher unemployment rate, especially if they have a non-Western background.
Megatrend 12: Resource scarcity	The ever-increasing global demand for resources (such as water, food, energy, land, and minerals) causes scarcity and inherent increases in costs. Global consumption has grown dramatically over the past century, impacting the demand for and use of natural resources and raw materials. Organizations increasingly need to rethink and tackle their dependence on scarce raw materials and resources. Finding new ways of working, innovating, and using alternative means and techniques is the key to survival for organizations. And if leaders don't respond with intrinsic motivation, society (and customers) will force them to minimize the negative impact of their organization on society and the environment.
Megatrend 13: Individualism	Individualism refers to the trend to distinguish oneself from another as a person, as an individual. This trend is a result of a shift from a collectivist society to a greater focus on the individual and society's increasing expectations about the availability of goods and services at any time and in the shape and form one desires. People and organizations increasingly expect tailor-made and personalized products, services, and solutions.

(Continued)

Table 2.1 (Continued)

Megatrend/ disruptor	Short description
Disruptor 1: Pandemics[10]	Pandemics place extraordinary demands on public health and medical care and threaten the functioning and even survival of organizations. Major outbreaks have serious, often long-lasting consequences for individuals, businesses, and society as a whole. The ensuing economic and fiscal effects—in the form of severe shocks to investment, production, and consumption—will last longer than the epidemiological consequences themselves.

Notes

1 Mittelstaedt et al., 2014
2 Naisbitt, 1982
3 Naisbitt and Aburdene, 1990
4 McGregor, 2012; Peciak, 2016
5 Cambridge Dictionary, 2020
6 National Intelligence Council, 2012
7 Van Dijk (2021)
8 Linthorst and Waal, 2020; Literature was marked as primary when it was based on practical research (such as a survey or interviews) and secondary if it consisted on an opinion of the authors.
9 If a source was addressing the future from one perspective or only focused on one megatrend/disruptor, it was marked as monodisciplinary. A source was marked as multidisciplinary if more than one discipline was involved—for example, if the future was discussed from a legal and an HR point of view and/or when it discussed multiple megatrends/disruptors.
10 Interestingly, we found only one disruptor mentioned in relation to the "future of work": the occurrence of a pandemic. Other possible disruptors, such as (nuclear) war (especially on a large scale), regional conflicts with global consequences (such as a war with Iran), infrastructural disasters (caused, for example, by foreign hackers), collapse of economic power blocs (such as the EU or China), or natural phenomena (such as solar geomagnetic storms) are discussed here and there in the literature but not specifically their implications for the future of work.

Chapter 3

The high-performance organization framework

To discover and develop courses of action to address the identified megatrends and disruptor, we used the HPO (high-performance organization) framework. An HPO—defined as an organization that achieves financial and non-financial results that outperform its peers/competitors over a period of five years or more by focusing in a disciplined manner on what is truly important to the organization[1]—is seen as an organization that can potentially thrive through disruption. This is because average-performing organizations generally have great difficulty addressing and managing disruptions, not to mention underperforming organizations. These disruptions regularly require an adapted or new business model and new ways of working. Many organizations do not have the required flexibility and change capacity to deal with this adequately. HPOs, on the other hand, are known for their flexibility and adaptability, which enable them to cope well with changing circumstances.[2] Thus, under most circumstances, they achieve organizational sustainability,[3] defined as the result of an organization's activities that demonstrate the organization's ability to maintain its business viability (including financial viability) without having a negative impact on social or ecological systems.[4] Our idea was that if we could develop practices that help HPOs better prepare for the future, these practices would undoubtedly be useful to other organizations, regardless of their performance levels.

It is, therefore, worth examining the impact of the identified megatrends and disruptor on HPOs. We do this by examining how each megatrend and disruptor affects the HPO framework we developed nearly twenty years ago.[5] We chose this particular framework to evaluate the impact of the megatrends and disruptor on organizations, as it is one of the few scientifically validated conceptualizations of HPOs.[6] Moreover, since its inception, the framework has been validated in numerous longitudinal (long-term) studies, showing that it is a useful enhancement technique for creating and maintaining HPOs over a longer period of time.[7]

DOI: 10.4324/9781003273264-3

3.1 The HPO framework: 5 factors and their 35 characteristics

The HPO framework was originally developed during a five-year research project based on data collected worldwide. It was then validated in practice with organizations for a further five years. The framework consists of 5 factors and their 35 associated characteristics (see Table 3.1).

Table 3.1   The 5 HPO factors and their 35 associated characteristics

HPO factor 1: Management quality
1. Management is trusted by organizational members.
2. Management has integrity.
3. Management is a role model for organizational members.
4. Management applies fast decision-making.
5. Management applies fast action-taking.
6. Management coaches organizational members to achieve better results.
7. Management focuses on achieving results.
8. Management is very effective.
9. Management applies strong leadership.
10. Management is confident.
11. Management always holds organizational members responsible for their results.
12. Management is decisive with regard to non-performers.

HPO factor 2: Openness and action-orientation
13. Management frequently engages in a dialogue with employees.
14. Organizational members spend much time on dialogue, knowledge exchange, and learning.
15. Organizational members are always involved in important processes.
16. Management allows making mistakes.
17. Management welcomes change.
18. The organization is performance-driven.

HPO factor 3: Long-term orientation
19. The organization maintains good and long-term relationships with all stakeholders.
20. The organization is aimed at servicing the customers as best as possible.
21. Management has been with the company for a long time.
22. New management is promoted from within the organization.
23. The organization is a secure workplace for organizational members.

HPO factor 4: Continuous improvement and renewal
24. The organization has adopted a strategy that sets it clearly apart from other organizations.
25. In the organization, processes are continuously improved.
26. In the organization, processes are continuously simplified.
27. In the organization, processes are continuously aligned.
28. In the organization, everything that matters to performance is explicitly reported.

29. In the organization, relevant financial and non-financial information is reported to all organizational members.
30. The organization continuously innovates its core competencies.
31. The organization continuously innovates its products, processes, and services.

HPO factor 5: Employee quality

32. Management inspires organizational members to accomplish extraordinary results.
33. The resilience and flexibility of organizational members is continuously strengthened.
34. The organization has a diverse and complementary workforce.
35. The organization grows through partnerships with suppliers and/or customers.

The five factors are described as follows:[8]

1. *Management quality*. HPO managers maintain trust with their employees by showing appreciation for their loyalty, treating them with attention and respect, and developing and sustaining good relationships with them. They encourage employees to have faith and trust in themselves and others, and they treat them in a fair and honest manner. They have integrity and act as role models for the employees and their colleague managers through their honesty, sincerity, dedication, enthusiasm, respectful attitudes, strong ethical values, credibility, and consistent behavior. They are not afraid to show their weaknesses, and they are neither complacent nor arrogant. They are also decisive. They avoid paralysis by analysis and propose quick and effective actions while stimulating others to also take action. HPO managers coach and facilitate employees in such a way that they can also achieve better performance. They offer support and assistance, and they protect their employees from outside influences when and where necessary. They are always approachable, but at the same time, they hold their employees responsible for their results and take corrective action when they do not perform well. They put their focus on achieving results, underline to employees that they are responsible for their own performance, and are not afraid to make difficult decisions (such as firing a person). They have an effective, self-assured, and strong management style that has been developed through the continuous communication of the values of the organization. They make sure that all their employees know the organizational strategy and support that strategy. Where necessary, HPO managers coach their employees in letting their own activities contribute to the achievement of the organizational strategy.

2. *Openness and action-orientation.* An HPO has an open culture, which means that there is a lot of dialogue between managers and employees and among the employees themselves to exchange knowledge and experiences, to increase commitment to the organization, and to create clarity on all organizational levels about what is important for the organization and what it wants to achieve. Managers explicitly ask for the opinions and ideas of their employees and act on that information. There is a lot of mutual respect, and everyone is asked to get involved in the important affairs of the organization. There is room for experimentation and failure in the organization, and there is no fear of taking (calculated) risks and making mistakes (as long as they are not repeated): these are seen as opportunities for learning. People give each other honest and sincere feedback with the goal of making things better, and this feedback is received as such. Knowledge is not power in an HPO, but shared knowledge is 1 + 1 = 3. The HPO culture is action-driven. There is plenty of deep thinking about issues, but HPOs do not suffer from paralysis by analysis. They do not overanalyze but balance thought with action. Thus, they take enough time for adequate decision-making and then quickly turn their decisions into actions to immediately solve problems. As a consequence, decisions can be made that are not optimal, and people understand that they may have to adjust a chosen course of action based on new information that becomes available.

3. *Long-term orientation.* For an HPO, long-term survival and contributions to stakeholders are much more important than short-term successes for shareholders. The organization and its people are extremely client-oriented: they listen carefully to what clients want and need, they understand the values and interests of clients, they build excellent long-term relationships with them, and they have regular direct contact with them. HPOs directly involve clients in the organization's affairs (such as the development of new products and services or the best way to perform new tasks). They are open to their reactions and aim to increase the value for clients. Their basic attitude is that every party that comes into contact with the organization should have a good feeling about the interaction because the organization added value and made things just a bit better for them, and if this is the case, it is only natural for the organization to exist as long as possible to make as many parties happy for as long as possible. The organization trains and grooms its people in such a way that new management can be promoted from within. Most managers have worked for a long time in the organization, albeit in different positions and possibly different locations, and thus know the organization, its stakeholders, its products and services, its employees, and

its industry very well. And because they are HPO managers, they can use this knowledge to good effect. HPOs are also a secure workplace, both physically and psychologically. Regarding the latter, people can make mistakes without having to be afraid of being fired. In fact, laying off people is the last resort for an HPO.

4. *Continuous improvement and renewal.* HPOs have a strategy that is unique either in content (what the organization wants to achieve) or in execution (how the organization does things) or (ideally) in both. This means that it is very clear to potential clients why they should go to this organization and not to other comparable organizations in the sector. An HPO also keeps developing new strategies to replace those strategies that are no longer unique or no longer working. The organization then does its utmost to put this unique strategy into practice. It improves, simplifies, and aligns the processes in the organization so it can act quickly and effectively on changing circumstances. Unnecessary procedures and tasks are removed, and information overload is combated. The organization does track the information that really matters by using critical success factors (CSFs) and key performance indicators (KPIs). It also precisely tracks whether objectives still contribute to the organization's strategy and goals and whether they are fulfilled. Difficult issues are immediately reported to both managers and employees so they can deal with them quickly and improve the way the organization is working. An HPO feels a moral obligation to continuously strive for the best results for its clients and its stakeholders. To this end, products, processes, and services are continuously improved and renewed. This is supported by a commitment to continuously strengthen the core competencies of the organization and its people.

5. *Employee quality.* An HPO has a diverse and, therefore, complementary workforce. New people are hired who already have HPO traits, such as a high degree of flexibility and the resilience needed to recognize and address organizational problems in a creative way. At the same time, these new hires will have different skills from the current workforce so that new competencies are continuously added to the organization's skill base. People are constantly developed through formal and informal training, on-the-job training, coaching, and working with other organizations. Regarding the latter, there is an explicit goal to create high-performance partnerships (HPPs). In this kind of environment, employees, with the support of their managers, seek to achieve extraordinary results for which they expect to be held accountable and receive feedback.

Our long-term HPO research shows that there is a direct and positive relationship between the five HPO factors and competitive performance: the higher the scores on the HPO factors (HPO scores), the better the organization performs; the lower the HPO scores, the lower the performance relative to the competition or comparable organizations. If an organization strengthens a specific HPO factor, it will have a positive effect on all other HPO factors. These are also reinforced and, in turn, have a positive influence on the other factors—and thus on the overall performance of the organization. Our longitudinal research also shows that the HPO factors and associated characteristics are robust over time. This means that they have hardly changed in recent decades and can, therefore, be regarded as *evergreens of excellence*.[9]

What versus how

The HPO framework does not include instructions or recipes that must be followed blindly. Managers and employees must translate the framework to the specific current situation in their own organization. So after the *what*, which is provided by the HPO framework (namely, we now know *what* we need to improve), the tailor-made improvement of the organization becomes the *how* (namely, *how* we have to improve differs per organization), which is taken care of by the organization itself. The HPO framework is, therefore, not a ready-made solution or recipe or blueprint for high performance. It indicates those areas in the organization that are important to be able to perform excellently. It is then up to managers and employees themselves to develop improvement initiatives to strengthen these areas.

End versus means

Becoming an HPO is not a goal in itself. It is a means for achieving the ultimate end: becoming an organization that is of the utmost value to its clients. The HPO framework helps you to develop a mindset and a way of thinking that achieves high performance in everything you do. This makes it possible to serve your clients as best as you can, and in the process, the organization becomes highly attractive to (potential) employees (by increasing their happiness at work) and, yes, achieves exceptional financial results.

Your organization can evaluate its high performance level and identify challenges and possible improvements by conducting an HPO diagnosis. The HPO diagnosis process starts with an HPO awareness workshop for management and other interested parties. During this workshop, the organization gets acquainted with the HPO framework, the HPO diagnosis, and the HPO transformation process. During the actual HPO diagnosis, management and employees complete the HPO question-naire, which consists of statements based on the 35 HPO characteristics. Respondents rate their organization on a scale of 1 ("we do not meet this characteristic at all") to 10 ("we fully comply with this characteristic") on these statements. The individual scores are averaged to arrive at scores on the HPO factors for the complete organization. These average scores indicate which HPO factors and characteristics the organization needs to improve to become an HPO. For these factors and characteristics, the organization drafts improvement actions that are incorporated into an HPO transformation plan. This plan is then executed during the year and updated when actions have been successfully wrapped up. The organization often installs an HPO champion and HPO coaches to guide this process. In principle, the HPO diagnosis is repeated every two years to evaluate improvements in both the HPO scores and the organization's performance and to identify new improvement areas.

3.2 Combining the megatrends and the disruptor with the HPO framework

To assess the impact of the identified megatrends and the disruptor on an HPO, we constructed a matrix in which we combined each megatrend and the disruptor with the characteristics of the HPO framework. For each of the thirteen megatrends and the disruptor, we analyzed whether they will influence each of the five HPO factors and their underlying characteristics, and if so, how. The matrix shows that the megatrends can influence the HPO factors both positively and negatively but that the disruptor mainly has a negative influence. In other words, some megatrends create oppor-tunities, while other megatrends and the disruptor mainly pose threats to organizations. In the following chapters, we have summarized these oppor-tunities and threats for each megatrend and the disruptor per HPO factor.

The cumulative consequences of megatrends[10]

Research by biostatistician Stein Emil Vollset shows that the expected decline in the world population, caused by women having fewer children, will have major consequences. It is true that two billion more people will be added worldwide in the coming decades, but at the same time, the average female fertility (the number of children she has) is declining rapidly: from 4.70 per woman in 1950 to 2.37 in 2017 to 1.66 in 2200. This development is due to the better education of women and greater access to contraceptives. In addition, the migration to the cities, which occurs mainly in developing countries, is reinforcing the declining number of children. After all, in the countryside children can help with the production of food, but in the city, that is not the case, and a child quickly becomes a cost.

The number of 1.66 is well below the replacement level of the existing population, so the world population will fall from a peak of 9.7 billion around 2064 to 8.8 billion in 2100. In 23 mainly Asian and European countries, the current population will more than halve. Mainly due to immigration, the US population will remain about the same as it is today, while India (1.1 billion) and Nigeria (790 million, up from 220 million now) will become the most populous countries in the world. Moreover, around that time, there will be twice as many people over 80 as children under 5 in the world. As a result, the classic population pyramid with few elderly people at the top and many young people at the bottom is turned upside down, so there will be fewer people who work than people who don't work. This raises questions, such as "Who is going to pay for all those pensions and healthcare expenses?"

For migrants, the scarcity in developed countries can help them gain a stronger position, with more rights. There will almost certainly be competition between Western countries for these immigrants. That battle will mainly be about the skilled workers because many of today's simpler jobs are being taken over by robots. The vastly different population size per country will influence the political and economic balance of power in the world. For example, China will first become the largest economy in the world but has relinquished that position to the US by the end of the century. The smaller number of people on earth can be good for nature and the climate, provided that humanity does not consume more than it already does.

In the next fourteen chapters, we discuss the thirteen megatrends and one disruptor separately and in relation to each other. For each megatrend/disruptor, we first give the definition and an explanation of it. We then describe the expected effects of the megatrend/disruptor on organizations and the future of work. Every megatrend/disruptor brings both opportunities and threats; we summarize what we found about this in the literature. Although we treat each megatrend/disruptor separately, in practice there is often a sometimes complex relationship between the megatrends and the disruptor: a megatrend/disruptor can strengthen or weaken the consequences of another megatrend/disruptor. For each megatrend/disruptor, it is indicated how it influences the other megatrends and the disruptor.

In addition to these substantive descriptions, in each chapter we pay attention to the question of how an organization can deal with the megatrend/disruptor. First, the self-assessment statements from the Futurize! diagnosis (see Chapter 18) are explained. With these statements, you can map out to what extent your organization is prepared for the impact of the relevant megatrends/disruptor to your organization. The statements emerged from an analysis of the megatrends and disruptor using the HPO framework. Finally, we give tips with which the organization can prepare for the relevant megatrends/disruptor. It is, of course, important to assess these tips and suggestions for suitability in the specific context of your own organization; they are not a list of activities that can simply be "ticked off." Each possible course of action should be assessed for expected impact in relation to the effort and costs involved.

Notes

1 Waal (2021)
2 Waal (2012)
3 Merriman et al. (2016)
4 Smith and Sharicz (2011)
5 Waal (2013)
6 Do and Mai (2020), Zbierowski (2020). Acording to Do and Mai (2020, p. 305) "in the HPO literature we only found the HPO framework developed by Waal (2012) as an example of a scientifically validated conceptualization of high-performance organizations."
7 Waal (2020), Waal and Goedegebuure (2017)
8 The descriptions of the HPO factors are taken from Waal (2020).
9 The HPO literature is by definition backward-looking, as researchers can only look at what organizations have done in the past to perform well. So the question was, do the characteristics of an HPO which were valid in the past also shape the HPO of the future? To answer this question, we examined whether the factors that create excellence, as found in the literature, were constant and stable over time. That is, can they, therefore, be assumed to be predictive of the future. In addition, research has been conducted into the way in which different generations of employees in an organization view and deal with the HPO framework. In this way, information was obtained on the longitudinal relevance and use of the characteristics in the HPO framework

(Waal, 2013; De Waal et al., 2017). The results of both studies show that, first, the HPO characteristics remain more or less constant over time (the *what*) and, second, that different generations view and attach the same importance to the HPO characteristics but use different means (the *how*) to strengthen these characteristics.

10 Straaten (2021)

Chapter 4

Speed of technological advancement

Megatrend 1

4.1 What is it?

Technological advancement is the collective term for the advancement of technological and digital tools, such as automation, big data, and advanced analytics, that increase productivity and provide better access to information and ideas. Organizations have been automating work for decades, but it is the increasing speed of change in technology that makes technological progress a force for change.

> In 2025, the time that man and machine spend on tasks at work will be equal.[1]

4.2 Some more explanation

Technological advances, coupled with the rapid pace of these advances, were most frequently cited in our research as having an impact on the future of work. Organizations have been working on technology and automation for decades, but it is the increasing speed of change in technology and automation that makes progress a huge force for change. With the risk that the explanation at the time of the publication of this book is already outdated due to this speed, we nevertheless make an attempt to list the various changes.

In the literature, this trend is also referred to as the fourth industrial revolution or Industry 4.0. Industry 4.0 is originally a German project dealing with the strategic approach to digitization and automation. The nine pillars of Industry 4.0 are[2]

1. the use of big data and advanced data analysis methods that influence decision-making in organizations;

DOI: 10.4324/9781003273264-4

2. the emergence of autonomous robots that have the ability to learn and perform specific tasks;
3. simulations, based on mathematical models, to optimize processes;
4. horizontal and vertical system integration, leading to smart factories;
5. the industrial Internet of things, connecting physical objects and systems;
6. the cloud, which makes it possible to work via shared platforms;
7. production methods, such as 3D printing, allowing for custom production;
8. augmented reality, enabling human-machine interaction; and
9. cybersecurity awareness, leading to the implementation of defense mechanisms to protect organizations from cyberattacks.

Nowadays, it is possible to buy digital fashion online and use it to beautify your Instagram or TikTok appearance. For example, the collections of Amber Jae Slooten, digital fashion designer and founder of digital fashion house The Fabricant, can only be worn digitally. In the design process of a collection, she does not touch any physical piece of fabric or clothing, and in her studio, there are only computers, so no more clothes racks with samples. This new fashion is doing well: in 2018, the Scandinavian brand Carlings sold out its collection of digital fashion within a month. The Fabricant rose to fame in 2019, when the fashion house sold a $9,500 dress to the wife of a Silicon Valley tycoon. The dress was custom-made on a photo of the owner, after which she posted this photo on social media.[3]

The digital artwork *Everydays: The First 5,000 Days,* by American artist Beeple, was recently auctioned for $69 million at Christie's auction house. The artwork includes a *non-fungible token* (NFT), a certificate of ownership linked to blockchain technology. This is a unique code through which the owner can claim to be the rightful owner of the digital work of art and also has the right to resell this work of art. Incidentally, it is not the case that an NFT file cannot be copied; that is still possible. But with an NFT, the owner buys the right to tell the outside world that he/she owns the "original," while others can have the same file at the same time. As *The New York Times* writes, you buy the right to brag about it.[4]

4.3 What are the consequences of the speed of technological advancement for organizations?

The impact of technological progress on organizations is huge, especially because the changes follow each other so quickly. Technological advances lead to changes in the work itself, the organization of work, and the type of leadership required in technologically advanced organizations.[5] On the one hand, employment within certain occupational groups is declining due to automation; this threat creates fear and insecurity among the employees affected. On the other hand, certain tasks are replaced by new tasks that require new skills. This leads to an increasing mismatch between skills needed in the workplace and skills present in current employees. In fact, this discrepancy is so great that it is a separate trend: mismatch in skills (see Chapter 6).

Recent advances in the fields of robotics and artificial intelligence (AI) not only are forcing humans to interact with machines but nowadays also create replacements for human workers, even in advanced jobs. Technological developments make it possible to work remotely so that less office space will be needed in the future. Employees will always have a need for contact; the remaining office space will take on the function of meeting space. New ways of working together require different forms of leadership, which also require new skills.

Technological developments are also changing the way organizations organize themselves and their networks with suppliers and customers. Technology enables the collection and availability of massive amounts of data, which in turn plays an increasingly important role in organizational decision-making processes. But this requires the organization to have sufficient technological awareness and knowledge to use the data in the right way. Integrity, compliance, and stricter legislation are important in this respect. After all, due to privacy legislation, organizations must demonstrate that they handle data from all kinds of sources correctly and securely. All in all, the rapid changes in technology have a huge impact on organizations and the market in which they operate. Failure to respond to this megatrend in time can lead to objectives not being achieved and organizations getting into serious trouble.

Chinese insurer Ping An uses the artificial-intelligence-based Superfast Onsite Investigation claims system. This system compares photos of vehicle damage to a database containing photos of 25 million parts of the 60,000 different car models and brands sold in China. The system then automatically calculates how much it will cost in parts and labor to have the damage repaired at a garage. The system also uses facial recognition to read customers' facial expressions, potentially detecting lying and cheating with false claims. In its first year of use, the system has helped Ping An settle seven million claims and save more than $750 million.[6]

4.4 What are the opportunities and threats?

According to our research, the megatrend speed of technological advancement creates opportunities as well as threats for organizations (see Table 4.1).

Table 4.1 The opportunities and threats

Megatrend	Speed of technological advancement
Opportunities	• New technologies can increase the effectiveness of management because they can have better and faster decision information. This is subject to the condition that managers act as role models by being technically skilled and implementing technological solutions in a safe manner together with their employees.
	• New technologies can significantly improve communication, dialogue, and knowledge-sharing processes, contributing to openness and action-orientation in the organization.
	• New technologies enable the organization to better serve its customers, provided that the organization handles data and security fairly.
	• New technologies have the potential to improve business processes and can even provide an organization with a unique advantage.
	• New technologies can reduce or replace heavy work or routine tasks, making work more interesting and sustainable for employees.
	• New technologies can be used in employee training.
Threats	• New technologies can become a threat to the quality of management if it is not sufficiently technically savvy and/or does not adequately deal with trust and security issues (data integrity and reliability of information).
	• With the rapidly changing technological environment, it is difficult to assess which technological innovations will suit the organization best and to foresee whether these innovations can be successfully implemented.
	• New technologies can cause anxiety, stress, and illness in employees who are insufficiently supervised and/or do not believe they can keep up with the changes caused by those technologies.
	• The reduction in routine chores (which causes a greater proportion of work needing brain attention) and the constant interruption and switching between tasks could lead to an increasing number of burnouts.

In 1995, the American economist Jeremy Rifkin predicted that the jobs of three in four workers would be lost because their work would be done by computers and robots. That actually turned out not to be the case. In fact, between 2000 and 2015, thanks to technological changes within organizations, the chance that employees would lose their job decreased by 1.7%. New technology offers many new possibilities, creating new jobs. In addition, organizations need to hire more people to implement new processes around that technology and to have cybersecurity and privacy rules in order.[7]

Summary proceedings were filed against a manufacturer of GPS watches because the app associated with the watch would entail the risk that privacy-sensitive data could end up in foreign hands. Rapid technological progress can, therefore, also (unexpectedly) lead to costs and challenges in the legal field.[8]

4.5 How does the speed of technological advancement affect the other megatrends?

Megatrends and disruptors do not stand alone but can, depending on the situation, strengthen or weaken each other's impact. How does the speed of technological advancement influence the other megatrends?

Technological progress allows for more flexible work and promotes globalization but, at the same time, causes an increasing mismatch in skills. This may increase social inequality. Automation can provide a solution to staff shortage and make work more sustainable, for example, when robots take over boring or heavy tasks. Furthermore, technological innovations enable personalized production and services, enabling an organization to better respond to increasing individualism. Finally, technological progress can play a role in detecting pandemics and/or taking measures against their further spread. An example of this is the corona app.

Experts expect that holidaymakers will combine the freedom of an individual trip with the security of an organized holiday. To facilitate this, travel organizer Sunweb is experimenting with dynamic packaging: a "travel agent robot" that tailors the holiday trip for the holidaymaker. Sunweb also has a "holiday doctor" app that allows travelers who fall ill while on holiday to contact a local doctor in their own language and a virtual tour guide that is available 24/7 for questions from the holidaymaker.[9]

4.6 Self-assessment

How well prepared is your organization for the future when it comes to the speed of technological advancement? With these statements from the Futurize! diagnosis (which we discuss in Chapter 18), you can determine for your organization whether it responds well to this megatrend. The statements have been developed by looking at the speed of technological advancement from the perspective of the five universal HPO factors. The corresponding HPO factor is given for each statement, and we explain why it is important to aim for a good score for the statement:

- *Management quality: Management is at the forefront when it comes to adopting new technologies.*

  Decisions about new systems and technologies are usually made by management. Insufficient knowledge and awareness of new technologies within management can lead to the organization not keeping up with the pace of innovation.

- *Openness and action-orientation: Employees are involved in the selection and implementation of new technologies.*

  When new technologies are selected and implemented together with employees, there is a greater chance that the most suitable technologies will be purchased thanks to the joint knowledge. The chance also increases that these will subsequently be successfully implemented and actually accepted and used by the employees

- *Long-term orientation: There is a clear organizational strategy (plan of approach and follow-up) for the application of new technologies.*

  Precisely because technological developments follow each other in rapid succession, it is important to formulate and implement a technology and ICT strategy. Due to the constant availability of innovative solutions, it is essential to use a process of exploring, experimenting, and innovating.

- *Continuous improvement and renewal: New technologies are used for the continuous improvement and renewal of processes, products, and/or services.*

  The rapid changes in technology offer many opportunities to innovate. It is important to seize these opportunities in order not to fall behind as an organization.

- *Employee quality: New technologies are carefully implemented, with attention to the necessary training and coaching of employees.*

  The benefits to be gained from new technologies stand or fall with the way in which the organization uses these technologies. It is, therefore, necessary that employees are adequately coached to develop the necessary knowledge and skills to deal with the new technologies. This increases the acceptance rate so that the desired benefits can actually be achieved.

Call centers are increasingly introducing technologies based on AI. For example, the Beyond Verbal application can analyze a customer's word choice and speaking style during a telephone conversation. The sales employee can then be informed whether this customer is an early adopter or a more conservative buyer. In the first case, the sales employee receives a signal to offer the customer the latest product; in the second case, mainly proven products are highlighted.[10]

4.7 How can you prepare?

How can you ensure that your organization is constantly up-to-date and well prepared to respond to the increasing speed of technological advancement? Several courses of action emerged from our research:

- Ensure sufficient tech savviness in the management team.
- Employees are also future users. So involve them in selecting and implementing new technologies so that the impact of these new technologies on them is not underestimated.
- Investigate in a timely manner which skills are required for the use of the new technologies.
- Tailor the required training and development of new technologies to the target groups within the workforce.
- Pay sufficient attention to ethics and safe use of new technologies and data.

A large container port, Cisco, ESRI, and IBM are building a digital twin of the port. These twins are an exact replica of the port's operational activities: the infrastructure, ship movements, weather, geographic data, and water conditions are monitored with 100% accuracy. Crucial objects, such as bollards and quay walls, will also record data about their status and environment. For example, digital bollards can provide insight into the condition and utilization of a berth and into the water and weather conditions in the area. Based on this, the harbormasters can determine the optimal time and place for a ship to moor. In addition, by predicting water and weather conditions, it is possible to determine how easily a ship can enter the port. With the help of machine learning, more and more knowledge is then gained based on patterns in the data. All this results in operational management that makes it possible for the port to increase the volume and efficiency of the goods transshipped while at the same time reducing environmental impact.[11]

Notes

1 Zahidi et al. (2020)
2 Erboz (2017)
3 Godwin (2019)
4 Heijink (2021)
5 Bhalla et al. (2017), Brougham and Haar (2018), Cook (2017), Gruen (2017), Healy et al. (2017), McQuay (2018), Ransome (2019)
6 Bhargava (2020)
7 Hofman (2021)
8 Piersma (2021)
9 Benjamin (2021)
10 Diamandis and Kotler (2020)
11 den Hartog-de Wilde (2019)

Chapter 5

Flexible employment
Megatrend 2

5.1 What is it?

Flexible employment refers to an increasing variation in work arrangements and practices—for example, in the number of working hours/times, work locations (such as working from home), and types of employment contracts. It is expected that traditional nine-to-five jobs will change to remote and on-demand work, as mobile technology and the Internet no longer require employees to work in the same fixed location. An increase in "liquid" positions and jobs is also expected, in which people will have multiple roles within one organization or work as independent contractors. This movement is called the gig economy or network economy.

> The text you are reading now started out as an audio file that the author recorded in Texas. It was then sent to the IBM Watson AI machine, which converted the audio into text. The file was then edited by a freelancer in South Africa (who won the contract in an online auction among a pool of freelancers around the world), after which the text was reviewed by a graduate research assistant in Washington, DC. The text was then printed and edited by the author in Texas and subsequently edited again by a freelancer in the Philippines. All these steps, which took place entirely over the Internet, represent the modern equivalent of the assembly line.[12]

5.2 Some more explanation

The traditional career in which an employee physically goes to the same workplace for many years and spends a fixed number of hours there to perform work is on the decline. Nine-to-five jobs are being transformed into mobile and on-demand work that employees, thanks to mobile technology and the Internet, no longer have to perform in the same physical

DOI: 10.4324/9781003273264-5

location (flex workers). The fixed definition of the term "job" is also changing. People increasingly have multiple jobs, fulfill multiple roles within an organization, or become self-employed, renting themselves out to organizations.[3] This movement is called the gig economy or network economy.[4]

Fast-growing firms facilitating this economy include digital employment platforms that outsource work through an open call to a geographically dispersed crowd (such as Upwork and Clickworker) and location-based applications that assign work to employees in a specific geographic area (such as Uber and Airbnb). Because of these platforms, a growing number of employees are no longer permanently employed by an organization but are hired for a specific task—only to say goodbye after completion. Although it is difficult to determine the number of people who work in this way, it can be assumed that this is work type is experiencing exponential growth.[5]

> The pace of change in today's society is such that it is no longer sufficient to prepare students for a professional life based on the idea of career as a stable and clearly defined path. The average graduate can expect to have held more than 11 different jobs before the age of 50.[6]

5.3 What are the consequences of flexible employment for organizations?

Flexible employment leads to a decrease in permanent and fixed-term employment contracts, in favor of an increase in self-employed contract workers. This can cause more uncertainty for (certain categories of) people and less loyalty of people to organizations. It will also become more common for employees to have contracts with multiple organizations at the same time, which can lead to more burnouts and more complex work planning for those people. Remote working is increasing, as is working on different days and hours, which requires different leadership styles from managers, more flexible work planning, and better communication and alignment.

Working remotely can both improve and deteriorate work-life balance. Employment contracts and job tenures are getting shorter, with the result that employees and managers are part of an organization for shorter periods. This may not benefit knowledge transfer and stability. The fact that fewer employees physically come to the office can save costs, but it does require more investment in communication technology. Flexible working leads to shorter tenures of both employees and managers, a greater variation in contracts, and challenges in the planning, organization, and stability of work and leadership. In addition, the legislation on flexibility and security is constantly changing, something that organizations must take into account and comply with (this also entails an increase in administrative work.)

Artemis Connection, a small strategy consulting firm in the Seattle area, was virtually born in 2015. Some employees have never met their colleagues in person. When building the virtual organization, one of its foundations was flexibility. That flexibility consists of scheduling work in 15- to 20-hour cycles. These cycles form the framework for both client projects and individual time commitments. "For example, we can estimate that a particular assignment, such as writing a weekly communications briefing, involves about 60 hours of work per week," said the founder and CEO, Christy Johnson. "That's four blocks, so then we need either two people who can do two blocks, or four who are going to do one." In addition, according to Johnson, people are given control over their work pace and the way in which they organize their work. For example, her own style is to do the thinking work in the early morning, so she arranges her schedule so that that part of the day is left free.[7]

5.4 What are the opportunities and threats?

According to our research, the megatrend flexible employment creates opportunities as well as threats for organizations (see Table 5.1).

Table 5.1 The opportunities and threats

Megatrend	Flexible employment
Opportunities	• The deployment of workers can move with the needs of the organization (in terms of number/costs and required skills). • Working from home/remote working can potentially save costs due to less travel and less office space required. • Flexible working hours and working from home or other locations can contribute to a better work-life balance.

(Continued)

Table 5.1 (Continued)

Megatrend	Flexible employment
Threats	• The increasing flexibilization of labor can jeopardize the quality and stability of management and employees in the organization. • Management has to make more effort to keep in touch with the growing group of flex workers. • It is more difficult to keep an increasingly large group of flex workers involved in the organization. They are potentially quicker to choose another, more attractive organization and, therefore, leave more easily. • Successive jobs and short-term contracts offer no (financial) security and can get people into trouble (financial problems, stress, burnout). • Employees may be afraid of losing their job, which can lead to a culture of fear. Errors in the work are then covered up and are more difficult to detect and fix. • With an increasing number of flex workers, it is becoming more difficult to involve employees in improvement processes. That is because management may not think it wise to involve the flex workers; because of their temporary nature, they may be more difficult to communicate with, or they may not stay long enough to get truly involved. • Flex workers as a group may receive less attention from management. This can lead to a less engaged workforce with lower quality and motivation.

5.5 How does flexible employment influence the other megatrends?

Megatrends and disruptors do not stand alone but can, depending on the situation, strengthen or weaken each other's impact. How does flexible employment influence the other megatrends?

The flexibility of the labor market can lead to more sustainable working conditions through a better work-life balance and the possibility to work remotely. Thus, flexible employment supports the preferences of employees, both in terms of the generation and the individual. But the same flexibility can also increase social inequality for employees who do not have enough work and/or struggle with low wages and lack of social protection.

Flexible work, especially obtained through platforms, can offer a solution for employees who cannot find a job in their home country or for organizations with labor shortages. It may even trigger a reverse reaction to urbanization and labor migration trends, as work can be done from rural areas through technological solutions. The same applies in times of disruption, such as the corona crisis: flexible employment gives both employees and organizations flexibility in numbers of employees and in working hours.

Home-based organizations need to become familiar with asynchronous (i.e., not real-time, thus with delays between participants responses) communication, such as via a Slack channel, a custom intracompany portal, or a shared Google doc. Geographically dispersed team members write their questions and comments and rely on team members in other time zones to respond at the earliest opportunity. An advantage of this approach is that employees share ideas, plans, and documents at an early stage and welcome early feedback; the pressure to present polished work is less than in the more formal, synchronous team meetings. At Zapier (a workflow automation company with more than 300 employees in 24 countries), the Zap Pal program pairs each new hire with an experienced buddy, who sets up at least one introductory Zoom call and then regularly contacts the rookie. For synchronous brainstorming, the company uses video calls and online whiteboards, such as Miro, Stormboard, IPEVO Annotator, Limnu, and MURAL, but it also encourages employees to use asynchronous methods to solve problems via Slack.[8]

5.6 Self-assessment

How well prepared is your organization for the future when it comes to flexible employment? With these statements from the Futurize! diagnosis (which we discuss in Chapter 18), you can determine for your organization whether it responds well to this megatrend. The statements have been developed by looking at flexible employment from the perspective of the five universal HPO factors. The corresponding HPO factor is given for each statement, and we explain why it is important to aim for a good score for the statement:

• *Management quality: Management treats flex workers, temporary workers, and freelancers the same as full-time employees.*

In an HPO, managers maintain a good and respectful relationship with employees, regardless of their background or level. If this does not happen, flex workers, temporary workers, and self-employed workers will be less motivated because they feel disadvantaged—with all the negative consequences for productivity and quality.

- *Openness and action-orientation: Flex workers, temporary workers, and freelancers are involved in the dialogue, knowledge, and learning processes.*

When the organization uses flexible working methods, it is important that flex workers, temporary workers, and self-employed workers, just like permanent employees, can participate in the discussion and learn within the organization. If this does not happen, the organization runs the risk that working methods are not known to everyone or that opportunities for improvement are not used because flex workers cannot provide input (ideas) or have insufficient knowledge to contribute to improvements.

- *Long-term orientation: There is a clear organizational strategy (plan of approach and follow-up) aimed at dealing with an increasing flexible employment.*

It is important for an organization to have a policy with regard to flexible employment and flex workers. In this way, fluctuations in work can be dealt with quickly and adequately, performance can be managed (remotely), and processes can be prevented from being disrupted as a result of the flexibilization.

- *Continuous improvement and renewal: The organization supports flexible employment (location, working hours, and multiple employers).*

It is expected that part of the future workforce will want to be able to work flexibly. Organizations can, therefore, better facilitate this instead of prohibiting it. This may mean adjustments in contract forms and stipulations in employment contracts and in home working applications. Organizations that do not go along with this trend run the risk of not being attractive enough for (future) employees.

- *Employee quality: The knowledge of flex workers, temporary workers, and freelancers is used in the improvement processes within the organization.*

The use of the knowledge that flex workers, temporary workers, and self-employed persons have will enrich the organization. A point of attention here is safeguarding that knowledge so that it also remains in the organization when the flexible employee leaves.

At GitLab, all team members have access to a "work manual" that now consists of 5,000 searchable pages and is effectively the central knowledge repository for the company. All employees are encouraged to add information to it regularly. They learn how to create a new topic page, edit an existing one, and embed videos. Prior to meetings, organizers post agendas linking to the relevant sections of the work manual so that participants can read background information and ask questions beforehand. After that, recordings of the meetings are posted on the GitLab YouTube channel, and the handbook is updated to reflect decisions made.[9]

5.7 How can you prepare?

How can you ensure that your organization is constantly up-to-date and well prepared to respond to the need for flexible employment? Several courses of action emerged from our research:

- Inventory the needs of employees and the required flexibility in the organization. Which employment conditions and contract forms are appropriate in order to achieve good alignment between the two?
- Keep an eye on the (ever-changing) legislation on flexibilization of work. Anticipate and respond to changes in a timely manner.
- Also involve the flex workers in the activities and learning programs of the organization.
- Invest in remote working, not only in the technology it requires but also in the ways of communication and leadership that come with working from home.
- Safeguard the knowledge of flex workers. Prevent the organization from becoming the victim of increasingly shorter contracts in which no or insufficient knowledge is built up and too little (lasting) improvement is achieved.
- Try to retain good flex workers, temporary workers, and freelancers for a longer period of time by offering them meaningful work and a pleasant work environment.

The boundary between what can be seen as a flex worker and an employee with a fixed contract is constantly changing. It is important as an organization to be aware of this and to respond correctly because negligent action is increasingly being addressed. For example, the court recently labeled Deliveroo's meal deliverers as employees: the company's construction to hire them as independent entrepreneurs was brushed aside.[10]

Notes

1 Ray and Thomas (2019)
2 Nice to mention in this respect is that the book *Futurize!* also came into being in a completely remote way. No physical meeting has taken place from the start of the research through the submission of the final manuscript to the viewing of the proof of the manuscript.
3 Anani (2018), Anthes (2017), Batt (2018)
4 Anani (2018), Anthes (2017), Batt (2018)
5 Howcroft and Bergvall-Kåreborn (2019)
6 Gallup en Bates College (2019)
7 Gratton (2020b)
8 Choudhury (2020)
9 Choudhury (2020)
10 Winkel (2021)

Chapter 6

Skills mismatch
Megatrend 3

6.1 What is it?

Skills mismatch refers to the expected gap between the current skills the workforce has and the skills the workforce needs for future jobs. Learning new skills to adapt to the changing work environment is not a new phenomenon, but with the increasing speed of change, it is seen as a challenge to prepare organizations, employees, and educational systems in a timely manner for the changing workplace. In addition, it is not yet entirely clear what these changes to the workplace entail and what new skills are required exactly.[1]

> Of the jobs that will exist in 2030, 85% have not yet been invented. Of all employees, 54% will have to be extensively retrained in the coming years.[2]

6.2 Some more explanation

The World Economic Forum states that the most in-demand professions or specialties in many industries and countries did not exist ten or even five years ago. In fact, the pace of change in occupations is even expected to accelerate.[3] Most literature, therefore, points to the need for organizations and employees to focus on lifelong learning. Only then can a smooth transition to new ways of working, new jobs, and other forms of employment contracts be guaranteed.[4] When it comes to the future of work, the focus is no longer just on college degrees but also on having the skills required for specific tasks.[5] Given the speed of change, skills and competencies—such as adaptability and agility, critical thinking, entrepreneurship, and interpersonal skills—are seen as essential for survival in the workplace.[6] At the same time, policymakers, educators, and education systems need to reshape to prepare for the new ways of working and the new skills required.[7]

DOI: 10.4324/9781003273264-6

Talent shortage is increasing worldwide, with the largest year-on-year increase in the shortage in the USA, Sweden, Finland, Hungary, and Slovenia. More than half of the world's organizations cannot find the skills they are looking for, almost double from a decade ago. Only 18% of countries currently report no talent shortage.[8]

6.3 What are the consequences of the skills mismatch for organizations?

Achievements in the past offer less and less a guarantee for the future. It is about the skills in the here and now, and these can change anytime. There is, therefore, a threat of a shortage of workers with the right skills and a surplus of workers with skills that no longer fit the jobs of the future. As a result, organizations can no longer deliver the required performance, which jeopardizes the continuity of these organizations.

As stated earlier, there is an increasing need for employees with skills, such as flexibility, adaptability, critical thinking, entrepreneurship, and interpersonal qualities. Teaching these skills is currently underrepresented in most school curricula. Organizations will, therefore, have to invest in training their staff themselves. This concerns more investment not only in educational programs but also in the people who organize and run these programs.

Many forward-thinking companies look for multifunctional experience when hiring new staff. For example, because its employees move from team to team and from role to role, Google prefers problem solvers with good cognitive ability over people who have role-related knowledge. When this rapidly evolving organization hires someone for a specific job, it needs to be sure that that person can easily do something else within Google the moment that job changes or expires. That comes down to hiring especially smart generalists.[9]

6.4 What are the opportunities and threats?

According to our research, the megatrend skills mismatch creates opportunities as well as threats for organizations (see Table 6.1).

Table 6.1 The opportunities and threats

Megatrend	Skills mismatch
Opportunities	• The increasing skills mismatch is forcing organizations to innovate in education and training. • Continuous attention to education and training leads to improvement of employee quality in the long term. • Investing in education and training gives the employee a sense of appreciation and motivates them to stay with the organization.
Threats	• Management needs to put in more effort to manage a workforce that increasingly lacks the right skills and qualifications. • The skills mismatch can also affect the management population and jeopardize the overall quality and stability of management. • The organization must ensure that even more and faster knowledge exchange takes place to compensate for the missing skills of employees. • Scarcity of skills may lead to an increase in labor costs. • Improvements are difficult to achieve with people who lack the right skills. • Communication and dialogue can become more difficult as management has to take into account the different skills of employees. • Education and training can become a goal in itself, whereby too little attention is paid to their impact on employees and the organization. • The feeling of insecurity, stress, and absenteeism can increase as a result of insufficient skills among employees. • The results of the organization can come under pressure due to the required investments.

More and more people are finding that their skills are outdated, making it difficult for them to get well-paid, good quality work—or any kind of work for that matter. In Europe, 43% of workers say they have recently experienced changes in the technologies used at work. One in five believe that current skills are likely to become obsolete in the next five years.[10]

6.5 How does the skills mismatch influence the other megatrends?

Megatrends and disruptors do not stand alone but can, depending on the situation, strengthen or weaken each other's impact. How does the skill mismatch affect the other megatrends?

The mismatch in skills requires new ways of training. Because flex workers generally participate in training programs less often than permanent employees, they need extra incentives to follow the necessary training. New technological innovations can play a positive role in this.

Having or not having the necessary skills and the opportunities available to develop these can increase social inequality. The mismatch in skills also has consequences for sustainable employability because employees with missing skills cannot deliver the required performance. This can lead to stress, burnout, and possible dismissal. However, it is also possible that investing in training and development motivates employees to stay longer with an organization.

> Technology is increasingly being used to train practical skills in real-life situations. For example, virtual reality is helping the plumbing and heating industry improve certification programs for mechanics. In the medical field, virtual resources are used to teach students how to communicate with patients and how to master advanced surgical procedures. UPS uses virtual training modules to prepare drivers for a variety of road hazards.[11]

The increasing social inequality, combined with the mismatch in skills, jeopardizes the availability of good and motivated employees. Organizations can expect to be encouraged by the government to provide equal opportunities in their programs.

6.6 Self-assessment

How well prepared is your organization for the future when it comes to skills mismatch? With these statements from the Futurize! diagnosis (which we discuss in Chapter 18), you can determine for your organization whether it responds well to this megatrend. The statements have been developed by looking at skills mismatch from the perspective of the five universal HPO factors. The corresponding HPO factor is given for each statement, and we explain why it is important to aim for a good score for the statement:

- *Management quality: Management skills are continuously aligned with the future needs of the organization.*
  To ensure that management has sufficient quality, it is important to structurally introduce and implement development plans for this group. If the quality of management no longer matches the strategy of the organization, it is wise to replace and/or strengthen certain roles within management in good time.
- *Openness and action-orientation: The organization is actively engaged in inventorying and developing the skills needed for the future (so that they are available in time).*
  An HPO continuously strives for the renewal of knowledge and skills on the basis of research and experiments; it is a learning organization. By continuously developing new skills, the organization is able to anticipate future changes in a timely manner and to remain a leading player in the market.
- *Long-term orientation: There is a clear organizational strategy (plan of approach and follow-up) to maintain the required skills in the organization.*
  An HPO continuously strives to increase its value for customers now and in the future. To achieve this, it continuously invests in developing the skills of its employees—not only in skills needed now but also in skills needed in the future.
- *Continuous improvement and renewal: Processes to acquire needed skills are continuously improved and renewed*
  People can acquire knowledge and skills in increasingly efficient ways. Combinations of learning on the job, online courses, gamification, and other forms of learning contribute to continuous improvement and renewal in this area. Organizations need to study and then choose from these innovations to determine how their employees can develop as efficiently and effectively as possible.

The Danish Technology Pact (Teknologipagten) is a partnership between the Danish government, the business community, and educational institutions, with the aim of ensuring that more people (especially young people) opt for technical and digital education. This will help to better meet the high demand from the private sector for skills and competencies in science, technology, engineering, and mathematics. The technology pact is a direct response to the shortage of workers with digital and technical competencies that is playing out across the country.[12]

- *Employee quality: Employee skills are continuously aligned with the future skill needs of the organization.*

  Just like managers, employees must have sufficient quality to be able to (continue to) perform their work. It is, therefore, important to agree and implement development plans for this group that are aligned with the strategy of the organization.

6.7 How can you prepare?

How can you ensure that your organization is constantly up-to-date and well prepared to respond to increasing skills mismatch? Several courses of action emerged from our research:

- When developing and updating the strategy and annual plans, pay attention to the development of the required skills and, therefore, to investing in these.
- Ask employees what skills they think they will need in the future. Match these with what the organization most likely needs and put together a learning and development program based on the matching results.
- Make learning needs a regular point of discussion in the dialogue with employees and ensure that specific, measurable, attainable, realistic, timebound (SMART) agreements are made in this area.

To help organizations address the challenge of growing skills shortages and skills mismatches, a new generation of talent platforms has emerged, such as Catalant, InnoCentive, Kaggle, Toptal, and Upwork. Unlike Uber, Amazon, Mechanical Turk, or TaskRabbit, these new platforms provide on-demand access to highly skilled workers. In doing so, they meet a great need: today, almost all Fortune 500 companies use one or more of these platforms.[13]

Cisco's Networking Academy provides IT training and skills development to students to prepare them for a wide variety of technical roles. The Academy then brings internal vacancies to the students' attention, as well as vacancies with external partners. Students benefit from better career development opportunities, while Cisco has a large pool of talent with specific skills that are a priority for the company.[14]

- Ensure adequate training budgets, especially when implementing new processes and systems.
- Distinguish in workforce analyses between required skills in the short, medium, and long term.
- Investigate existing methods and programs that suit the organization, such as a lifelong learning program, a skills passport, or the exchange of knowledge and/or employees with other organizations.

Notes

1 Kochan (2019), Lent (2018)
2 Ratanjee (2020), World Economic Forum (2018a)
3 World Economic Forum (2018a)
4 Cassells et al. (2018), Healy et al. (2017)
5 Kasriel and Upwork (2018)
6 Bakhshi et al. (2017), Fuller et al. (2019), Illanes et al. (2018)
7 Bakhshi et al. (2017), Harteis (2018), Lund et al. (2019)
8 Manpower Group (2020)
9 Mansharamani (2020)
10 Whiteley and Casasbuenas (2020)
11 Bhargava (2020)
12 Whiteley and Casasbuenas (2020)
13 Fuller et al. (2020)
14 Smet et al. (2021)

Chapter 7

Sustainable employment

Megatrend 4

7.1 What is it?

Sustainable employment (or similar concepts, such as sustainable work and decent work) refers to the extent to which employees want and can continue to work at the organization now and in the future.[1] It is about providing work and working conditions that keep employees happy, healthy, and motivated. There is increasing attention and concern among management about the impending workforce shortage due to the aging workforce and changing job demands of new generations. A growing awareness of sustainability in general among the population and also among the organization's customers plays a role in this.

In cities in developing countries, many workers depend on the informal economy for a job. For example, in the largest cities in Latin America, 50 to 60% of youth employment consists of jobs in the informal economy. Even under informal working conditions, young workers receive training and gain work experience, earn more than minimum wage, even have more savings than employees in the formal sector, and feel positive about their work experience. However, the informal sector offers few opportunities for more advanced on-the-job skills development. Most informal occupations make minimal use of the skills relevant to success in the "official" labor market, and skills that are not used can quickly deteriorate. In Latin American cities, only one in six jobs in the informal sector requires a high level of cognitive skills, compared to one in three in the formal sector.[2]

DOI: 10.4324/9781003273264-7

Having meaningful work is especially important for the younger workforce. Compared to older generations, millennials are more likely to derive meaningful purpose from their work than from other sources. Four out of five graduates confirm the importance of finding purpose in their work. However, less than half of graduates manage to actually find that meaningful work. That's a problem because it turns out that graduates with meaningful work are almost ten times more likely to experience high well-being.[3]

7.2 Some more explanation

Concerns about sustainable employment are fueled by the fact that in many (Western) countries there is an (imminent) staff shortage as a result of the aging of the labor population and the changing demands of new generations in regard to work (such as that this must have a purpose). In addition, awareness is growing among the population—and, therefore, among customers of organizations—for the sustainability of organizations' operations and decent working conditions for everyone.[4] As a result, more and more organizations are consciously working on creating sustainable working conditions. They also require this from their suppliers and customers, which has to be demonstrated through certification.

Unilever promises that all employees of suppliers who supply goods and services directly to the company will earn a living wage by 2030, even if it costs the company more. In addition, Unilever purchases more from entrepreneurs from underrepresented groups, such as women and ethnic minorities. According to the company, consumers do not have to worry about paying more.[5]

7.3 What are the consequences of sustainable employment for organizations?

The increasing focus on sustainable employment is leading to greater awareness among organizations and subsequently to programs for healthier working conditions, increased vitality, more sustainable employability, inclusiveness, meaningful work, and more opportunities for self-development. Organizations must offer a safe working environment and working conditions and pay more attention to the vitality and well-being of employees. Employees also demand challenging and meaningful jobs that lead to self-fulfillment. Organizations must invest more in the (personal) development of employees and be aware of issues such as gender equality and equal pay. All this has a positive effect on the performance and happiness of employees and will also lead to the recruitment and retention of high-quality employees.[6] On the other hand, neglecting society's sustainability expectations can lead to burnout, reduced engagement, or even the departure of employees and thus a decrease in the performance and results of the organization. This can jeopardize the continuity of the organization.[7]

> Transgender people often experience stigmatization, discrimination, hostility, and pressure to suppress their identity in social situations, including the workplace. Despite the growing awareness worldwide of this struggle, many employers are hardly developing policies and workplace cultures that support trans workers. The main reason for tackling this problem anyway is that it is simply the right thing to do. No person who works hard and contributes to the success of an organization should ever feel stigmatized and afraid of coming to work. In addition, not applying trans-specific policies can entail high costs for companies. Think of increased churn, decreased engagement and productivity, potential lawsuits, and damage to the company brand.[8]

7.4 What are the opportunities and threats?

According to our research, the megatrend sustainable employment creates opportunities as well as threats for organizations (see Table 7.1).

Table 7.1 The opportunities and threats

Megatrend	Sustainable employment
Opportunities	• The general trend of sustainable employment practices can strengthen trust in management. • A sustainable working environment that also takes the climate into account will attract and retain the stakeholders and employees who find this important. • Making work more sustainable leads to healthier and more involved employees who can be deployed better and for longer. • A CSR (corporate social responsibility) policy attracts employees and flex workers who are motivated to work for this type of organization.
Threats	• Management has to take creating sustainable working conditions and complying with associated regulations more into account. • The increasing pressure to demonstrate and implement policies on sustainable employability leads to extra work.

"In my view, the discussion should not be about permanent and
flexible, but about work that is well and poorly arranged. We have
quite a lot of poorly organized work in the country and I think that
is a social problem. Badly arranged work is that you deliver meals
on a bicycle or work in the catering industry without insurance.
It's called platforming, but it's not. It's pseudo self-employment.
Another example is poorly arranged work via a temporary employment formula, where the rules regarding safe work, wages and
insurance are not respected."[9]

7.5 How does sustainable employment influence the other megatrends?

Megatrends and disruptors do not stand alone but can, depending on the
situation, strengthen or weaken each other's impact. How does sustainable employment influence the other megatrends?

Organizations that prioritize sustainable work and sustainable employability may be better able to manage the skills mismatch and respond to
the changing composition of the workforce. This is because this prior-
itizing leads to easier attracting and retaining high-quality employees.
Sustainable employment and employability policies are expected to have
an effect on decreasing inequality.

Organizations can make work more sustainable by making it more flexible. For example, they can offer their employees opportunities for flexible working hours and locations, thus making a positive contribution to
work-life balance. Flexibility can also lead to less-sustainable conditions,
however, because it can lead to job insecurity and unrest among employees.

Making work more sustainable is also associated with environmental
issues. Both are aimed at sustainable value creation, and it is, therefore, in
society's interest that both are tackled at the same time. Due to advancing
globalization, there is increasing awareness and attention for working conditions in all parts of the world. Global agreements, such as the United Nations
Sustainable Development Goals, contribute to this attention (and hopefully
also to improvements). As a result, more and more attention is being paid to
the working conditions of labor migrants and to social inequality.

PepsiCo introduced a program in the past decade called Performance with Purpose. It is based on four pillars:

1.   Delivering superior financial returns (financial sustainability)

2. Transforming the product portfolio by reducing sugar, salt, and fat in the products while offering healthier, more nutritious foods and drinks (human sustainability)
3. Limiting the impact on the environment by saving water, reducing the ecological footprint, and reducing plastic waste (environmental sustainability)
4. Supporting people by providing new forms of assistance to employees' families and to people in the communities to which the organization provides products (talent sustainability)

Since the program was launched, revenues from healthier options have grown to 50% of total sales, water use in production has been reduced by 25%, and safe drinking water is supplied to 22 million citizens. R&D investment nearly tripled to expand nutritious offerings and minimize environmental impact.[10]

7.6 Self-assessment

How well prepared is your organization for the future when it comes to sustainable employment? With these statements from the Futurize! diagnosis (which we discuss in Chapter 18), you can determine for your organization whether it responds well to this megatrend. The statements have been developed by looking at sustainable employment from the perspective of the five universal HPO factors. The corresponding HPO factor is given for each statement, and we explain why it is important to aim for a good score for the statement:

- *Management quality: Management sets a good example in the field of sustainable working.*
  Sustainable work requires attention and policies in the field of flexible working hours, behavior, acceptance of mistakes, and a healthy lifestyle and work-life balance. Management must not only make time in order to achieve this themselves but also to really propagate these standards and values. When acting as a role model, a sustainable work culture will emerge within the organization.
- *Openness and action-orientation: The organization measures how working conditions are experienced by employees.*
  By measuring how the work and working conditions are experienced, the organization gains ideas about what works and what does not work (sufficiently). Based on this, new or additional measures can be taken. It is, of course, important that the measurement results are converted into concrete improvement actions.

- *Long-term orientation: There is a clear organizational strategy (plan of approach and follow-up) to promote sustainable employment.*

  Having an approach and strategy is necessary for a healthy organization in the long term—not only because healthy and satisfied employees perform better but also because organizations increasingly have to be able to demonstrate that they have and follow a strategy for this (think of quality marks such as fair trade).

- *Continuous improvement and renewal: The organization is continuously improving and renewing working conditions.*

  Because working conditions are continuously improving (think of a safe working climate, attention to health, and more operational and decision-making freedom), employees are better able to perform. In this way, the organization is and remains attractive as an employer.

- *Employee quality: Within the organization, sufficient attention is paid to the physical and mental health of employees.*

  By continuously paying attention to the sustainable employability of employees, an organization maintains its quality and health. These employees then remain motivated and committed to the organization, which leads to less absenteeism due to illness. In addition, employees like to continue working for an organization that invests in them.

There is a strong tradition of social partnership at HHLA, a leading European logistics company based in the Port of Hamburg, Germany. Social dialogue is used as a means to properly anticipate the introduction of new technologies in the workplace. By giving employees a voice in the onboarding process and involving employee representatives in this process, a culture of openness to innovation and learning new skills has developed within the company. Social dialogue at HHLA has prevented the potential adverse effects of new technology on employees and facilitated its introduction. This gave the company a clear competitive advantage.[11]

7.7 How can you prepare?

How can you ensure that your organization is constantly up-to-date and well prepared to respond to the need for sustainable employment? Several courses of action emerged from our research:

- Offer employees meaningful work, appropriate to their talents, and provide adequate training and support. Let them think about how their work contributes to the goals of the organization.

- Implement a sustainable employability program that focuses on, among other things, the mental and physical health of employees.
- Provide dignified and safe working conditions and fair wages, not only for your own employees but also for those of suppliers and customers.
- Investigate the wishes and needs of employees by periodically conducting employee surveys, entering into dialogue with employees, and organizing work and focus groups. In addition, a delegation of employees, such as the works council, can often provide valuable information about what is going on within the organization.
- Involve employees from different backgrounds in organizational initiatives so that their voices are heard.
- Communicate and/or promote to stakeholders (employees, customers, shareholders) that sustainable work is important to the organization.

Proponents of "alternative work arrangements"—many of which are powered by platforms like Uber and TaskRabbit—say these arrangements are a way to trade unemployment, burnout, and aversion to work for freedom, flexibility, and financial gain. Skeptics point to unstable earnings, little or no disability benefits, reduced job security, and stagnating career development. For people with desired (in-demand) skills, the gig economy often means a more exciting and entrepreneurial lifestyle. However, for the uneducated who turn to work in the gig economy out of necessity, it is only the best of the bad options. Financial uncertainty is a major and ever-present concern to them. In addition, when someone is controlled by an algorithm that sends notifications to their phone—without human interaction—it becomes more difficult to build relationships with bosses or coworkers, when these relationships could have helped them advocate better working conditions.[12]

Notes

1 United Nations (2019a), World Economic Forum (2018a, 2018b), De Jonge and Peeters (2019)
2 Sanchez-Reaza et al. (2018)
3 Gallup en Bates College (2019)
4 Annunziata and Bourgeois (2018)
5 FD (2021a)
6 Waal and Wit (2018)
7 Lange (2019), Dignan (2019), MacEachen (2018), Cook (2019)
8 Thoroughgood et al. (2020)
9 Jacques van den Broek, bestuursvoorzitter Randstad, in Pelgrim en Rijlaarsdam (2021)
10 Nooyi and Govindarajan (2020)
11 Global Deal (2020)
12 Torres (2018)

Chapter 8

Continued globalization
Megatrend 5

8.1 What is it?

Globalization is the process by which organizations develop international influence or operate in an international environment. An alternative description of globalization is the growing interaction and integration between people, companies, and governments worldwide. This trend is not new but is expected to continue in the near future. In light of the COVID-19 pandemic, which caused global problems in manufacturing and logistics, there is a slightly emerging trend of deglobalization. We see this especially with crucial products that countries want to produce internally. However, it is still unclear whether this movement will continue.[1]

> Globalization is probably the long-term trend that has the most impact on the future of jobs and work. We live in a highly connected and interdependent world—and this trend is only expected to increase over time—where no country has a monopoly on innovation and job creation. Globalization and technological change have created a complex economic and financial system characterized by interdependence and interconnectedness. For the first time in history, these interconnected systems are truly global, which also means that disruption in any part of the system will impact economies around the world. The recent global financial and health crises illustrate this.[2]

8.2 Some more explanation

During our research, we noticed that the occurrence of "globalization" as a megatrend in the literature was often mentioned together with the megatrends "speed of technological advancement" and "flexible employment." This suggests that there is a strong connection between these three trends. We have not found a recent source that focuses solely on

DOI: 10.4324/9781003273264-8

globalization as a megatrend or on the impact of globalization on the future of work, beyond the impact on organizations already mentioned under technological advancement and flexible employment. We conclude from this that the possible consequences of globalization are the same as those we have mentioned with regard to the speed of technological advancement and flexible employment.

8.3 What are the consequences of continued globalization for organizations?

Due to international conditions, ongoing globalization is leading to changes in the work itself, in the organization of work, and in leadership. Opportunities arise to solve the staff shortage by using external employees (flexibility). Remote working is becoming easier with innovative technological solutions but also presents new challenges when it comes to work planning and supervision. In addition, employees need social networks and meeting places. All this requires a different setup of the internal organization and communication.

Globalization of work requires new skills, which can lead to a feeling of insecurity and fear of job loss among employees and management. Working internationally requires new leadership styles and management skills, such as technological insight (necessary for working online) and new ways of communicating (necessary for dealing with cultural differences). Organizations have access to more (international) data and advanced analysis tools, which means that decision-making processes have to be set up differently. Organizations should, therefore, invest in training and retraining programs. If they cannot keep up with the pace, their continuity is in jeopardy.

Another point we want to consider regarding globalization is compliance with the ever-changing labor laws in the home country and in the other countries where an organization operates. A deteriorating economy and the lack of social protection can lead to undesirable working conditions for employees. Customers and stakeholders will increasingly ask for demonstrable proof that the organization plays an exemplary role in this.

Finally, it has to be mentioned that because of globalization, organizations can find themselves operating in countries with a volatile and precarious political environment, where sometimes even (civil) war breaks out. This not only makes doing business in a sustainable and safe manner (for the employees) difficult, but it also raises the question for management (beforehand) whether the organization should be in these countries at all.

A major US industrial equipment company built a new factory in China using the designs of its US and Japanese factories and then introduced them in China with improved equipment, newer equipment, and modified ways of working. The result was a streamlined operation, much more efficient than those in the United States or Japan. When the company built a next new factory in the United States, it repeated that process, now using lessons learned from the Chinese factory.[3]

8.4 What are the opportunities and threats?

According to our research, the megatrend continued globalization creates opportunities as well as threats for organizations, (see Table 8.1).

Table 8.1 The opportunities and threats

Megatrend	Continued globalization
Opportunities	• The pool of potential employees is growing. • Globalization can lead to a more diverse workforce. • The chances of a larger market share are increasing. • The organization can realize advantages as a result of increased scale. • Working with different cultures requires new skills (which is an opportunity because it stresses that lifelong learning is essential).
Threats	• Management needs to make more effort to keep in touch with employees who work all over the world. • Workforce diversity due to globalization requires increased management attention, as well as new ways and processes to meet different employee needs. • An increasing global playing field makes it more difficult to maintain good relationships with the many types of stakeholders and customers. • Working with different cultures requires new skills (which is a treat if employees are unwilling or unable to timely acquire these skills). • The fact that people come from different cultures makes communication, dialogue, knowledge exchange, and performance orientation more challenging because (cultural) misunderstandings are easy to occur (however, in the end, making use of a more collective intelligence will benefit the organization). • To remain relevant and competitive in a globalized market, the organization must find a unique strategy and support it with the best processes. • Organizations must take into account increasing complexity and costs in order to (be able to continue to) compete internationally. • Complying with local laws and regulations requires the necessary attention and expertise within the organization (which may then have to be sourced externally causing additional costs).

The coronavirus crisis has made society aware that globalized supply chains are quite vulnerable to disruptions. Over the past two decades, China and India have emerged as the main producers of active pharmaceutical ingredients (APIs), the workable components of medicines. Even before the corona crisis, there were regular shortages of medicines in Europe, mainly due to the strong dependence on a few large API manufacturers in Asia. A fire or pollution in a factory or a corona crisis immediately leads to large shortages in Europe. There is now a great consensus in the European Union that the system needs to be changed—for example, by producing medicines in Europe again, building a wider network of suppliers, or having factories make multiple types of APIs.[4]

8.5 How does continued globalization influence the other megatrends?

Megatrends and disruptors do not stand alone but can, depending on the situation, strengthen or weaken each other's impact. How does continued globalization affect the other megatrends?

The speed of technological progress is fueling globalization by increasing the number of technological solutions and opportunities to enable remote working. Globalization means that many products and services are manufactured in different parts of the world, which means that there is increasing attention—especially among the general public—for sustainable working conditions and practices in those parts of the world. In addition, globalization has consequences for the composition of the workforce of organizations. Possible shortages of skills and availability can be compensated by obtaining knowledge and manpower from other countries (labor migration).

Thanks to globalization, there is more attention for an integrated and global approach to environmental issues. The increase in international contacts, on the other hand, has a negative effect on the spreading risks of diseases (pandemics, as recently as COVID-19) and on the availability of certain imported goods. Driven by the desire to solve global environmental problems, there is a growing interest in purchasing more products from local suppliers, especially when it comes to critical goods.

According to Anna Hallberg, the Swedish foreign trade minister, deglobalization is an illusion: "While the COVID pandemic has shown how extremely dependent we have become on each other in the world, we cannot turn back the clock. Instead, we have to accept this dependence and deal with that situation." According to Hallberg, it is an illusion that the words "autonomous" and "trade" can go together: "The pandemic has shown that we need to better protect ourselves against health crises, for example by building up larger stocks. But that is different from wanting to become 'autonomous' or to start reshoring."[5]

8.6 Self-assessment

How well prepared is your organization for the future when it comes to continued globalization? With these statements from the Futurize! diagnosis (which we discuss in Chapter 18), you can determine for your organization whether it responds well to this megatrend. The statements have been developed by looking at continued globalization from the perspective of the five universal HPO factors. The corresponding HPO factor is given for each statement, and we explain why it is important to aim for a good score for the statement:

- *Management quality: Management reflects the composition of the global workforce.*

  To take advantage of the opportunities of globalization, it is important that management thinks and works globally. If this is not the case, there may be a mismatch between management's views and what is really happening in the different countries and cultures where the organization operates.
- *Openness and action-orientation: The organization facilitates global communication and interaction with and between employees from all parts of the world.*

  Creating a global workforce is one thing. In order to achieve good cooperation between all employees in that workforce, explicit attention is needed for intercultural communication and mutual coordination. In this way, the organization prevents miscommunication and misunderstanding due to differences in language and culture.
- *Long-term orientation: There is a clear organizational strategy (plan of approach and follow-up) to respond to advancing globalization.*

  It takes a lot of time and energy to enter markets in other countries or to respond to players from other countries entering the home country of the organization. In order to prepare the organization for this in good time, it is important to develop both a structured long-term approach and a flexible short-term approach.

- *Continuous improvement and renewal: Processes, products, and/or services are continuously aligned with the needs of local markets.*

    It is precisely a globally operating organization that must be aware of the fact that "one size fits all" does not hold. Therefore, it must ensure that the products and services delivered—although most likely based on a unified design—are adapted to the local markets where the organization operates, both in terms of content and the way the product/service is delivered.

- *Employee quality: Employees are able to communicate well with colleagues and customers from all parts of the world.*

    In addition to the technological tools, the workforce needs to have the right skills to work together. Mastering foreign languages and knowing cultures and local customs are essential for good cooperation and avoiding misunderstandings.

8.7 How can you prepare?

How can you ensure that your organization is constantly up-to-date and well prepared to respond to the continued globalization? Several courses of action emerged from our research:

- Create a diverse workforce that reflects the customers, markets, and cultures with which and in which the organization operates.
- Continuously research which opportunities and threats are occurring on a global scale and how other organizations worldwide are dealing with these in general and are locally. Where can you find the knowledge you need? How do other organizations solve certain problems?
- Participate in surveys and networks to gain knowledge.
- Also, stay locally oriented: prevent your organization from becoming too dependent on solutions that have to come from far, especially if these are business-critical.

Disruptions and shortages during the COVID-19 pandemic exposed the weaknesses in global supply chains. Many companies had not rigorously identified and addressed these vulnerabilities and were, therefore, basically caught out. The solution: thoroughly analyze your supply chain to discover the risks in it, identify alternative sources of supply in different locations, increase inventories of critical materials, review your product strategies, and explore new manufacturing technologies that can increase your organization's agility and resilience.[6]

Notes

1 Guttal (2010)
2 Pompa (2015)
3 Shih (2020)
4 Bokkum and Kuiper (2021)
5 Wiel (2021)
6 Shih (2020)

Chapter 9

Changing workforce composition

Megatrend 6

9.1 What is it?

The changing composition of the workforce is caused by both the aging population and the generational shift. Older workers are continuing to work longer than before for a variety of reasons. The generational shift also results in major changes in the composition of the workforce. The baby boomer generation will be replaced by the millennials, followed by generation Z and generation A. By 2025, millennials will make up the largest part of the workforce.

In 2015, the global workforce (people aged 15 to 64) was 4.8 billion people. By 2100 it will be 6.7 billion, but this expansion is uneven. More-developed regions will lose about 36 million workers over the next decade, and that loss will double by 2050 and more than triple by 2100. Upper-middle-income countries (Latin America, Middle East, North Africa, Asia) lose nearly 110 million workers by 2050, and at the end of the century, that loss could approach half a billion. Workforce growth will be almost evenly distributed between lower-middle-income and low-income countries; 85% of those new employees will work in sub-Saharan Africa. Two regions will represent 91% of all new workers in the world: West Africa (Burkina Faso, Cameroon, Ivory Coast, Mali, Niger, Nigeria) and Central Africa (Angola, the Democratic Republic of the Congo, Kenya, Madagascar, Mozambique, Tanzania, Uganda).[1]

9.2 Some more explanation

According to United Nations data, by 2050 one in six people in the world will be older than 65, compared to one in eleven in 2019.[2] Older workers are not only an increasing part of the workforce; they are also working longer. Older adults plan to work longer for a variety of reasons, such

DOI: 10.4324/9781003273264-9

as concerns about preserving benefits and income for healthcare and a desire to stay active and engaged because they will live longer than previous generations.[3]

In addition to the aging world population, the generational shift plays a major role in the composition of the working population. The shift from baby boomers and generation X (1960–1970) to millennials (generation Y, 1980–1990) and then to generation Z (2000–2010) and generation A (2010 and beyond) is leading to major changes in the composition of the labor force.[4] By 2025, millennials will make up the majority of the workforce. Although it appears from the literature that there is a difference of opinion about the precise effects on the future of work of these changes in the workforce, there is a unanimous opinion that different generations have different interests and, therefore, different needs.

> The longer people live, the longer they are expected to work. Individuals with multiple careers will become the new normal. Students now out of high school are expected to hold at least 11 different jobs between the ages of 18 and 42, a number that could easily double over a lifetime. According to Reid Hoffman, founder of LinkedIn, organizations no longer offer lifelong careers but rather a tour of duty: temporary assignments that give employees new skills, experiences, and training, which they can take and use on their next "tour." Therefore, lifelong learning becomes very important for the workforce: upskilling is crucial to remain competitive in the labor market. Organizations are forced to rethink career paths and are expected to facilitate the process of lifelong learning.[5]

9.3 What are the consequences of the changing workforce composition for organizations?

In general, the workforce is aging, and organizations must, therefore, ensure that successful aging can take place at work through, for example, vitality and well-being programs for older workers. Younger generations entering the workforce are more sensitive to sustainability, climate change, and purposeful and varied work. To attract and retain them, organizations must create (more) meaningful and sustainable work, with sufficient learning opportunities, sufficient variety in work tasks, and personalized working conditions. In short, organizations must be prepared for the diverse needs and wishes of different generations. Thus, the changing workforce composition requires better working conditions to ensure successful aging at work and to meet the needs of the younger generations. This is crucial to avoid a shortage of employees (retention of employees).[6]

In the coming years, organizations will have multiple generations working simultaneously: baby boomers, generation X, and millennials, working side by side. Such a workforce not only challenges previously established notions of hierarchy and seniority but also requires a specific set of management skills to manage and facilitate collaboration and learning across generations. The multigenerational workforce will also create friction: the typical jobs for young people—especially undergraduates—are dwindling. These jobs are filled by older, more experienced workers, who themselves suffer from the disappearance of jobs that require an average level of education. This development affects unskilled young people for whom the only route to the formal economy is through a series of temporary or part-time jobs. Because older, permanent employees enjoy legal protection, temporary employees (usually young people) have a greater chance of being fired. At the same time, older workers believe that young people have an advantage in the digital age, as they have grown up with the major changes and advancements in technology. Young people, on the other hand, argue that their career opportunities are being jeopardized by the older generation. In short: frictions are everywhere.[7]

9.4 What are the opportunities and threats?

According to our research, the megatrend changing workforce composition creates opportunities as well as threats for organizations (see Table 9.1).

Table 9.1 The opportunities and threats

Megatrend	Changing workforce composition
Opportunities	• Different generations bring a diversity of employees and, thus, also a diversity of skills, knowledge, ideas, and insights into the organization.
Threats	• There is a threat of a shortage of good quality personnel (including managers), which can put pressure on organizational results. • Increasingly aging management may miss the connection with new generations of employees. • Younger generations tend to stay shorter with an employer, which hinders long-term orientation (including promotions within the organization). The organization must make an extra effort to remain attractive to these generations and to cultivate a long-term orientation (culture). • Older employees and employees with special needs require more management attention and new ways and processes to deal with these requirements.

"The good news is that there is still a lot of work to be done. Due to technology and an aging population, there are major staff shortages. We have a very active investment agenda in this country: climate, infrastructure, building homes. And we want to be attractive to foreign investors, especially in tech. Over the next ten years, we will therefore be short of about 100,000 people in sectors where there is scarcity. The country will have to guide workers from shrinking professions, such as administrative jobs, to those growth professions with intensive personal guidance. If you do not intervene much more aggressively than now, you will get higher unemployment and labor shortages. That is the challenge facing all Western societies."[8]

9.5 How does the changing workforce composition influence the other megatrends?

Megatrends and disruptors do not stand alone but can, depending on the situation, strengthen or weaken each other's impact. How does the changing workforce composition affect the other megatrends?

The changing workforce is one of the reasons why the labor market is becoming more flexible: younger generations prefer more freedom in their work and prefer shorter and more flexible contracts. In addition, the shift in generations is also related to increasing individualism because younger generations grew up in an era in which great emphasis was placed on individual development and, thus, individualization. Younger generations are also more aware of the purpose and footprint of organizations and increasingly want to work for organizations that care about the planet. Organizations can attract and retain high-quality employees by paying more attention to this. They can then leverage the interests and skills of the younger employees by involving them in environmental issues and corporate social responsibility.

Organizations need to pay more attention to the needs of the different generations working within the company and the aging workforce. That is why sustainable employability is an increasingly important theme. Continued globalization ensures that organizations become less dependent on the availability of employees in the immediate environment of an organization. The changing workforce composition is also impacting cross-border immigration and urbanization, as immigrant workers can, on the one hand, solve the labor shortage and, on the other hand, cause the shortage of workers in countries or regions where they left from.

Finally, there is a link between the aging workforce and pandemics, as the older workforce is more vulnerable to disease. Organizations will, therefore, have to take more precautions to minimize the effects of a pandemic.

> The aging workforce means that developed countries must source workers from other countries or rely (even) more on automation. Even in a scenario where automation continues to replace workers in repetitive tasks and AI reduces the demand for workers with non-repetitive tasks, the demand for migrants is likely to remain high.[9]

9.6 Self-assessment

How well prepared is your organization for the future when it comes to the changing workforce composition? With these statements from the Futurize! diagnosis (which we discuss in Chapter 18), you can determine for your organization whether it responds well to this megatrend. The statements have been developed by looking at the changing workforce composition from the perspective of the five universal HPO factors. The corresponding HPO factor is given for each statement, and we explain why it is important to aim for a good score for the statement:

- *Management quality: The composition of the management reflects the ages and diversity of our workforce.*
  By making sure the composition of management reflects the composition of the workforce, the organization prevents a mismatch between what management thinks is going on and what is actually going on within the organization. A diverse management can better empathize with the different groups of employees and respond better to their needs. Moreover, a diverse management is an incentive for all types of employees to grow. (Managers are exemplary here.)
- *Openness and action-orientation: The organization leverages the diversity of its workforce.*
  Exploiting the diversity of the workforce provides added value to the organization in a number of ways. Diversity in people produces diversity in ideas and, with it, innovation. Employees who feel accepted and valued in their diversity are more motivated to commit to the organization and stay longer. If employees can develop on the basis of their own strength and diversity, they provide more valuable input for the organization.
- *Long-term orientation: There is a clear strategy (plan of approach and follow-up) for continuous improvement and renewal of the workforce.*

By thinking ahead and developing a (strategic) plan to respond in time to the future demand for employees, the organization will not be faced with any surprises in the future with regard to the availability of high-quality employees.

- *Continuous improvement and renewal: The organization ensures a good mix and balance between the generations of employees who work in the organization (strategic personnel planning).*

Organizations that have a diverse workforce with a good balance between generations have the opportunity to view improvement and innovation initiatives from all possible perspectives. This allows the organization to respond optimally to future developments and to align these with the working methods, knowledge, and skills of both current employees and employees of the future.

- *Employee quality: The organization takes into account a changing composition of personnel in education, training, and coaching.*

In order to guarantee employee quality in the future, it is important to take into account the different ages, learning styles, cultures, and levels of knowledge of the generations working in the organization. Otherwise, education and training may be less effective, and employees will not develop optimally. This ultimately comes at the expense of the quality of the organization. Thinking of the future shortage, it could be wise to invest in education in regions where workforce growth is expected. And in combination with growing inequality, to ensure education for children who normally do not have the possibility to learn (offer free education programs, start diversity programs in education institutes).

CVS, a major US drugstore chain, developed the Caremark Snowbird program, which allows older employees to transition to different CVS regions on a seasonal basis. Reasons for this were

- the expected shortage of younger workers due to changes in the demographic composition of the population,
- the recognition that the demographic makeup of customers is also changing: the customer base in many regions increasingly consists of older adults (and older employees can respond effectively to the needs of those customers), and
- retaining skilled, experienced adult employees who now make up more than 17% of CVS Caremark's workforce.

The Caremark Snowbird program is proving particularly popular among workers moving to Florida from the north during the winter.[10]

9.7 How can you prepare?

How can you ensure that your organization is constantly up-to-date and well prepared to respond to the changing workforce composition? Several courses of action emerged from our research:

- Map out the composition of the workforce and actively aim for a good mix of generations for the organization.
- Implement a sustainable employability program to maximize returns of employees regardless of their age.
- Investigate the wishes and needs of the employees by, for example, regularly conducting employee surveys and continuously entering into a dialogue with them.
- Involve employees of different generations in organizational initiatives in order to get the most possible ideas and acceptance.

Walmart, where 75% of current store managers started as employees, seeks leadership talent in places that are usually overlooked. The company has established more than a hundred Walmart Academies in its Supercenters. These academies provide leadership and management development training to employees who have just been promoted to supervisory positions, such as department heads. And sometimes that path goes all the way to senior leadership, as the example of the current COO of Walmart US shows. He started working at a Walmart in Oklahoma at age 17 after his dream of playing college football went up in flames due to a broken hip. Incidentally, that first job was arranged for him by his mother, herself a Walmart employee.[11]

Notes

1 Sanchez-Reaza et al. (2018)
2 United Nations (2019a)
3 De Lange (2019), Rudolph et al. (2018)
4 Appel-Meulenbroek et al. (2019), Hyder (2014)
5 Pompa (2015)
6 Bhalla et al. (2017), Campbell et al. (2017), Jayne et al. (2017), Kubicek and Korunka (2017)
7 Pompa (2015)
8 Jacques van den Broek, CEO Randstad; in Pelgrim and Rijlaarsdam (2021)
9 Sanchez-Reaza et al. (2018)
10 Sloan Center on Aging & Work (2012)
11 Ingram (2021)

Chapter 10

Increasing inequality

Megatrend 7

10.1 What is it?

Concerns about increasing wage and income inequality in the world are growing.[1] While employment rates did increase overall (pre-corona) globally, there are several groups of workers who did not and still do not benefit in equal measure.[2] Their situation also appears to be deteriorating—especially low-skilled workers, employees with jobs that are in danger of disappearing due to automation, self-employed persons/self-employed persons (gig workers), and employees with a migration background are at risk. In addition, the gender gap (which also leads to wage differences) is not expected to disappear in the near future.[3]

Multinationals and market-driven capitalism have generated tremendous growth since World War 2, significantly reducing world poverty. However, this growth has not benefited everyone. In developed economies, a small segment of the population has reaped the most gains, while many working-class people in rural and especially urban communities have experienced a socioeconomic decline. In the developing world, the situation is even worse. While growth has raised living standards in Africa, Asia, and Latin America, more than a billion people still live in extreme poverty and outside the formal economy. This is especially the case in countries with a large rural population. Here small farmers are excluded from the supply chains to large food companies because they lack knowledge of modern agricultural practices and have no money for new technologies anyway. Developing countries also face massive shortages of human talent and skilled labor.[4]

DOI: 10.4324/9781003273264-10

10.2 Some more explanation

Growing inequality has led to an increasing need for social protection for vulnerable workers, with measures ranging from legal protection in flexible working arrangements to the introduction of a universal income.[5] Legal protection in flexible working arrangements means that contract workers receive the same income as employees with the same tasks who have a permanent contract. In Finland, as a social experiment, a universal basic income was introduced in 2017. Unemployed residents between the ages of 25 and 58 receive an unconditional monthly basic benefit. This is not only a solution to poverty but also seems to save the government from bureaucratic enforcement of the law. As a result of increasing inequality, according to the literature, more government policies should be introduced to eliminate inequality and protect vulnerable workers.

The Oxfam report *The Inequality Virus*, on economic inequality in the world, shows that nine months after the outbreak of the corona pandemic and the accompanying economic recession, the wealth of the thousand richest people in the world has already returned to pre-corona levels. At the same time, corona has increased income inequality in the world, which hinders the fight against global poverty. Oxfam expects that by 2030, the number of people living in poverty (i.e., living on less than $5.5 a day) will reach 3.3 billion: 500 million people more than before the pandemic.[6]

Between 1982 and 2020, the number of billionaires in the United States has grown almost fiftyfold (from 13 to 614), according to the business magazine *Forbes*, with the richest of the rich also getting richer. This increase has two main causes: corporate politics and government policy. In terms of corporate politics, shareholder capitalism has caused revenues at the top to soar, while the lower levels of the organization have not benefited. They are also increasingly at risk of losing their jobs. With regard to government policy, it appears that the richest Americans pay the least taxes.

10.3 What are the consequences of increasing inequality for organizations?

Poverty and inequality trigger all sorts of other problems, such as health problems and poor performance. Financial problems or job insecurity "gets into one's system." Not only the whole family suffers from this situation; work and society suffer too. Increasing inequality is, therefore, expected to lead to government policies that provide (extra) protection for certain groups of employees. Under the new legislation, organizations will have to organize training programs for low-skilled workers, which can provide these workers with sustainable employment. In addition, organizations must offer equal wages and sustainable working conditions. Diversity should no longer play a role in this. Organizations will have to demonstrate that they invest in the development of their employees and treat them all equally. In addition to the necessary investments, this new legislation may also entail an increasing administrative burden.[7]

Racism and discrimination are much more common than many people suspect because they don't necessarily have to be deliberate, premeditated acts. They just happen. For example, research shows that applicants with "white-sounding" names are on average 50% more likely to be invited for an interview than applicants who are equally qualified but have a "black-sounding" names. Moreover, a white skin color equates to eight extra years of work experience. Many black and Asian applicants, therefore, "whitewash" their CV by, for example, adopting a less ethnic-sounding name or not mentioning activities that indicate an ethnic identity. This indeed has a "positive effect" on the chance of being invited, even among employers who say they have a strong preference for diversity.[8]

Open hiring is a new recruiting method invented in the United States. In this case, someone who wants to work puts his or her name on a list, and in the event of a vacancy at one of the participating organizations in the open hiring program, the person top on the registration list immediately starts working without further fuss. As a result, the background and past of the applicant play virtually no role in the selection for a job. The employers who participate in the program are mainly socially involved entrepreneurs who do not want to exclude anyone and who, due to the nature of their work, can offer almost everyone a workplace. The program also appears to be a solution to staff shortage, as many more people are eligible to fill an open vacancy.[9]

10.4 What are the opportunities and threats?

According to our research, the megatrend increasing inequality creates opportunities as well as threats for organizations (see Table 10.1).

Table 10.1 The opportunities and threats

Megatrend	Increasing inequality
Opportunities	• When the theme of inequality is put on the agenda of the management team, it will lead to interventions on their part, which means an improvement in life for everyone. After all, management must ensure that all employees have equal opportunities. As a result, those employees will become extra motivated for the organization, with all the positive consequences that entails. • The organization can positively distinguish itself from other organizations by setting up special programs aimed at vulnerable groups.
Threats	• An increasingly narrow talent pool of employees is emerging because fewer people have the opportunity to be properly trained. • More investments are needed to keep employees affiliated with the organization. • Management must take into account the different needs, skills, and prospects of specific groups of employees while at the same time avoiding the exclusion of vulnerable groups from these processes. • The organization must ensure the protection of vulnerable (migrant) worker groups to minimize staff turnover and maximize performance. • There is an increase in legislation and regulations to promote equality of opportunity. Organizations must demonstrate that they contribute to this.

Organizations that rank in the top 25% in terms of gender diversity in their management team are 21% more likely to have above-average profitability than companies in the bottom 25%. In terms of ethnic diversity, companies in the top quartile are 33% more likely to outperform in terms of profitability. The argument for diversity is convincing: diverse companies are more successful companies.[10]

A well-known cause of pay differentials, low retention, and stalled career progression for women, people of color, and especially women of color is bias and discrimination in hiring, professional development, and promotions. However, something can be done about that. When hiring, push for targeted recruitment within minority groups. This prevents your organization from becoming dependent on referrals based on a network of personal contacts. These have been convincingly demonstrated to maintain the homogeneity of the workforce. Ensure that candidate pools are diverse, including at least one person from a minority group. Make sure that discussions of the recruitment and promotion committee are fair, and be aware of "red flag comments." Examples of these include "*His* resume is really impressive," "Sounds like *she's* a busy mom," "I'd like to see evidence from *her* that she can handle this responsibility before we promote her," and "I'm not sure whether *she* is a good fit for that position." Such language often serves to exclude (colored) women. You can respond with something as simple as "Would we have made these comments about a (white) man?"[11]

10.5 How does increasing inequality influence the other megatrends?

Megatrends and disruptors do not stand alone but can, depending on the situation, strengthen or weaken each other's impact. How does increasing inequality affect the other megatrends?

Megatrends such as speed of technological progress, flexibilization of work, and increasing skills mismatch can lead to social inequality for workers who are underemployed and/or struggle with low wages and lack of social protection. By allowing organizations to invest in training for these vulnerable groups, sustainable working relationships can be built.

Increasing social inequality is further linked to cross-border immigration and urbanization. Migrant workers and specific groups of workers in rural and/or urban areas are more vulnerable. Because they are away from their own culture, family, and friends, they enjoy less (social) protection and experience more stress. Investments in training, good working conditions, and equal working conditions (no distinction based on gender or nationality) can also lead to sustainable employment here.

Technologization leads to inequality among vulnerable groups in society. Lower-skilled workers who have worked for the same company for more than ten years, workers over the age of 50 and first-generation migrants with a non-Western background are particularly affected by new technologies. In addition, they are less likely to find a new job when they leave a company. This is because they need new skills from a potential new employer, which they do not or insufficiently possess. More consideration should, therefore, be given to how technological change can be designed in such a way that as many people as possible benefit from it and do not further increase inequality.[12]

10.6 Self-assessment

How well prepared is your organization for the future when it comes to increasing inequality? With these statements from the Futurize! diagnosis (which we discuss in Chapter 18), you can determine for your organization whether it responds well to this megatrend. The statements have been developed by looking at increasing inequality from the perspective of the five universal HPO factors. The corresponding HPO factor is given for each statement, and we explain why it is important to aim for a good score for the statement:

- *Management quality: Management takes active action against increasing social inequality.*
  To combat social inequality, it is important that management plays an exemplary role by, for example, actively combating inequality in terms of employment or setting up special training programs for vulnerable groups of people/employees.
- *Openness and action-orientation: Management assesses policy decisions against the impact on vulnerable groups of people/employees.*
  If an organization wants to get the most out of its employees, it is important to combat inequality of opportunity. This can be done, among other things, by testing intended decisions against the impact on vulnerable groups and by discussing policy decisions with the relevant employees.
- *Long-term orientation: There is a clear organizational strategy (plan of approach and follow-up) to promote equality of opportunity in the organization.*
  As a result of the increasing inequality of opportunity, the availability of suitable employees is decreasing. A good training strategy

with a specific focus on different target groups offers a solution for reducing inequalities in the field of development opportunities.

- *Continuous improvement and renewal: The organization has special initiatives to support vulnerable employees.*

  In addition to a strategy, exemplary behavior and impact assessment of policy plans, special initiatives, and budget are needed to offer vulnerable employees opportunities. In this way, the organization can respond flexibly to current issues and tackle acute (feelings of) inequality.

- *Employee quality: The organization deploys its own employees to stimulate the development of vulnerable colleagues.*

  The deployment and development of vulnerable employees require more attention and resources. In that sense, they should not be treated equally but should receive extra attention. All employees within the organization can contribute to this by, for example, setting up guidance programs or organizing internships for their vulnerable colleagues.

The social class from which a person comes has a cultural effect that is lasting. American workers from lower social classes (who, because of the location of their crib, have relatively less access to money, social contacts that can promote their upward mobility, and cultural know-how needed to get ahead in schools and companies) are 32% less likely to become a manager than people from a higher social class. This is not only detrimental to individuals but also to organizations and society. For individuals, it is a disadvantage as it significantly reduces their career potential and general well-being. It is disadvantageous for organizations because a group that possibly produces above-average leaders is excluded. For example, a study in the US military showed that individuals from a lower social class are less self-centered than those from a higher social class, making the former more effective as leaders. Similarly, a UK study found that lawyers without an elite background are more motivated and capable than their privileged peers. The class disadvantage is detrimental to society because it means that many workers do not have the opportunity to contribute optimally to economic growth. To better deal with the disadvantages of social class, companies must emphatically add social class to their diversity goals.[13]

10.7 How can you prepare?

How can you ensure that your organization is constantly up-to-date and well prepared to respond to increasing inequality? Several courses of action emerged from our research:

- Hire workers who are in a vulnerable position or at a distance from the labor market and invest in them.
- Make contacts with local training institutes and discuss which students have the potential to grow but are hindered by certain circumstances. Give them a chance by, for example, offering internships.
- Develop training programs for vulnerable employees in the organization together with specialists.
- Allow employees from vulnerable groups to contribute ideas and decisions about their training and development.
- Show understanding and patience for vulnerable groups of employees. Organize more support for them by, for example, appointing a permanent mentor or coach.

Organizations spend millions each year on anti-bias and anti-discrimination training, with the goal of creating a diverse workforce. Research shows that diverse groups outperform homogeneous groups, are more involved, have higher collective intelligence, and are better at making decisions and solving problems. Unfortunately, research also shows that bias prevention programs rarely deliver results. While bias itself is hard to eradicate, it's not that hard to limit. Here are some tips:

- Create a diverse pool of candidates. Whether you work with recruiters or hire staff yourself, make it clear from the start that you want true diversity, not just one female candidate or one minority candidate.
- Establish objective hiring criteria, define culture fit, and demand accountability from your managers for the candidates they hired.
- Base interviews on skills-based questions. Ask every applicant the same questions and make each question directly related to the knowledge and skills you need. Assess the conversations immediately; this way, you can compare candidates fairly on the basis of predetermined criteria and avoid favoritism.

- Carefully assign people to high-value projects. Respond to possible double standards and stereotyping: pay close attention to the way people in your team talk about their colleagues and how they behave in groups. Make sure all types of people can have their say.
- Schedule inclusive meetings where everyone is welcome and able to attend. Business meetings should take place in the office, not at a golf course or college club. Otherwise, you favor people who are more comfortable in those environments or people whose personal interests overlap with yours.
- Stick to regular working hours where possible; otherwise, you run the risk that caregivers and others with demanding private lives will not be able to participate in activities.[14]

Notes

1 Balliester and Elsheikhi (2018)
2 Annunziata and Bourgeois (2018)
3 Peetz (2019)
4 Kaplan et al. (2018)
5 Colombino (2019)
6 Kalse (2021a)
7 Behrendt and Nguyen (2019), Bell et al. (2017), Florito et al. (2018), Kiss (2017), Doorn (2017)
8 Livingston (2020)
9 Wienen (2021)
10 CBI (2020)
11 Melaku et al. (2020)
12 Hofman (2021)
13 Ingram (2021)
14 Williams and Mihaylo (2019)

Chapter 11

Environmental issues
Megatrend 8

11.1 What is it?

Environmental issues concern changes, and their consequences, in the global climate caused by human activities.[1] Floods, sea-level rise, forest fires, extreme weather events, and natural disasters caused by climate change lead to major disruptions to everyday life. Climate change is expected to have a huge negative impact on future economic growth, as significant investments need to be made to reduce the carbon footprint of people and businesses, promote sustainability, and protect the environment. There is also the question of how to deal with the expected migration of people from countries with the greatest environmental issues.[2]

Scientists are observing changes in the Earth's climate in every region and across the whole climate system, according to the latest Intergovernmental Panel on Climate Change (IPCC) Report. Many of the changes observed in the climate are unprecedented in thousands, if not hundreds of thousands of years, and some of the changes already set in motion—such as continued sea-level rise—are irreversible over hundreds to thousands of years. However, strong and sustained reductions in emissions of carbon dioxide (CO_2) and other greenhouse gases would limit climate change. While benefits for air quality would come quickly, it could take 20–30 years to see global temperatures stabilize.

The report provides new estimates of the chances of crossing the global warming level of 1.5°C in the next decades and finds that unless there are immediate, rapid, and large-scale reductions in greenhouse gas emissions, limiting warming to close to 1.5°C or even 2°C will be beyond reach. The report shows that emissions of greenhouse gases from human activities are responsible for

DOI: 10.4324/9781003273264-11

approximately 1.1°C of warming since 1850–1900 and finds that, averaged over the next 20 years, global temperature is expected to reach or exceed 1.5°C of warming. This assessment is based on improved observational data sets to assess historical warming, as well progress in scientific understanding of the response of the climate system to human-caused greenhouse gas emissions.

The report projects that in the coming decades, climate changes will increase in all regions. For 1.5°C of global warming, there will be increased heat waves, longer warm seasons, and shorter cold seasons. At 2°C of global warming, heat extremes would more often reach critical tolerance thresholds for agriculture and health, the report shows. But it is not just about temperature. Climate change is bringing multiple different changes in different regions—which will all increase with further warming. These include changes to wetness and dryness, winds, snow and ice, coastal areas, and oceans. Below are some examples:

- Climate change is intensifying the water cycle. This brings more intense rainfall and associated flooding, as well as more intense drought in many regions.
- Climate change is affecting rainfall patterns. In high latitudes, precipitation is likely to increase, while it is projected to decrease over large parts of the subtropics. Changes to monsoon precipitation are expected, which will vary by region.
- Coastal areas will see continued sea-level rise throughout the 21st century, contributing to more frequent and severe coastal flooding in low-lying areas and coastal erosion. Extreme sea-level events that previously occurred once in 100 years could happen every year by the end of this century.
- Further warming will amplify permafrost thawing and the loss of seasonal snow cover, melting of glaciers and ice sheets, and loss of summer Arctic sea ice.
- Changes to the ocean, including warming, more frequent marine heatwaves, ocean acidification, and reduced oxygen levels, have been clearly linked to human influence. These changes affect both ocean ecosystems and the people that rely on them, and they will continue throughout at least the rest of this century.
- For cities, some aspects of climate change may be amplified, including heat (since urban areas are usually warmer than their surroundings), flooding from heavy precipitation events, and sea-level rise in coastal cities.

The report also shows that human actions still have the potential to determine the future course of climate. The evidence is clear that CO_2 is the main driver of climate change, even as other greenhouse gases and air pollutants also affect the climate. Stabilizing the climate will require strong, rapid, and sustained reductions in greenhouse gas emissions and reaching net-zero CO_2 emissions. Limiting other greenhouse gases and air pollutants, especially methane, could have benefits both for health and the climate.[3]

11.2 Some more explanation

Due to the expected impacts of climate change, there is a growing awareness among customers about the environmental footprint of organizations they do business with. As a result, increasing pressure is being put on governments by them to enforce clean and sustainable value creation. This requires more and continuous innovation of production methods and solutions for resource depletion by organizations (see also Chapter 15 on resource scarcity). The population, customers, and stakeholders demand visible measures to absorb the negative consequences of the (business) processes for the environment. In this regard, the so-called triple bottom line is a concept worth mentioning: a recommendation for organizations to ensure sustainable value creation, focusing as much on social and environmental issues as on profit.[4]

According to scientists from the University of Cambridge and the British Bird Conservation Service, the economic value of nature reserves is seriously underestimated. The researchers calculated for a number of natural areas what they yield if they are or remain for nature and what they yield if they are used for agriculture or forestry. In most cases, nature conservation gives a higher return, to which the advantage of preserving biodiversity must also be added. The greatest economic return is achieved by preventing climate change; beneficial effects are also achieved with regard to coastal protection, pollination, harvesting of wild plants, protection against flooding, clean drinking water, and recreation.[5]

11.3 What are the consequences of the environmental issues for organizations?

Environmental issues are forcing organizations to rethink the way they create value so that they can achieve sustainable development goals and provide decent (sustainable) work. Existing production and supply of goods and services can be endangered by their negative effects on the environment. Organizations should not only increase awareness of their ecological footprint but also actually invest in clear and sustainable value creation. The entire value chain in which the organization operates has to be involved in this. Investments in innovation are, therefore, necessary. As customers and stakeholders become increasingly aware of environmental issues, they are asking organizations to take visible measures. If this does not happen, they will refuse to buy from or cooperate with organizations that do not (want to) work in a sustainable way. This has a negative effect on the results, which can jeopardize the continuity of the organization.[6]

Millennials, in particular, make purchasing decisions based on sustainable and eco-friendly brands and products, with the result that their brand appreciation has more than doubled over the past decade. This trend is confirmed by the growing number of eco-friendly or sustainable startups reaching successful maturity. Tony's Chocolonely, a company that was founded as a niche supplier of "slave-free" chocolate, is now the number one seller of chocolate in the Netherlands in terms of turnover. Manufacturer Alpro, with its range of plant-based drinks, yogurt, cream alternatives, and desserts, has experienced the largest market share growth in the dairy category in Europe. To contribute to the achievement of the ambitious CO_2 targets from the Climate Agreement, the construction industry will increasingly exchange traditional materials, such as concrete and steel, for relatively low-emission raw materials, such as wood, bamboo, and flax. This makes the residential area of the future made of wood.[7]

This is the outdoor retailer Patagonia's mission: "Patagonia is in business to save our planet." The company has donated millions of dollars to environmental causes in recent years, came up with the idea of recommerce (where customers can exchange used equipment for a voucher) and has a website where customers can track products from the production line to shipping to the stores.[8]

11.4 What are the opportunities and threats?

According to our research, the megatrend environmental issues creates opportunities as well as threats for organizations (see Table 11.1).

Table 11.1 The opportunities and threats

Megatrend	Environmental issues
Opportunities	• Visible interest of an organization in strengthening sustainability and improving the environment can increase the confidence of customers and employees in the management of that organization. • A sustainable work environment that also takes the climate into account will attract and retain stakeholders and employees who care about this. • Climate change will lead to more sustainable innovation and renewal.
Threats	• Management has to spend a lot more time taking into account the consequences of their decisions and actions on climate change. • Environmental issues will require a lot of consultation and process improvement capacity. • To remain relevant and competitive, the organization must find a unique strategy and support it with processes that do not negatively impact the climate.

The lack of intergenerational responsibility (thinking about the consequences of one's own actions for future generations) is a Western phenomenon. In other cultures, the long term is much more central. Several original inhabitants of the United States, such as the Iroquois and the Dakota, are familiar with the concept of seventh-generation thinking. This means that every decision that is made is tested against the question: does this benefit the seventh generation that follows us? The concept of *whakapapa* is central to the Maori in New Zealand: everyone is part of a chain of life that comes far from the past and reaches far into the future. When making a decision, all previous and future generations watch along. In Japan, municipalities involve residents when making big plans. The residents are randomly divided into two groups: one group of residents looks at the consequences of these plans for today, and one group of residents does the same for 2060. It turns out that the 2060 group is opting for much greener and healthier plans.[9]

The good news is that more and more companies want to lead the way with products and services that provide solutions to the consequences of the climate crisis. For example, investors of soap and food producer Unilever will vote for the first time on the group's climate policy at the next annual meeting. The bad news is that it is still difficult for companies to quantify exactly what the concrete consequences are of rising sea levels and more extreme weather and how climate change and policies will affect the living and working environment.[10]

11.5 How do environmental issues influence the other megatrends?

Megatrends and disruptors do not stand alone but can, depending on the situation, strengthen or weaken each other's impact. How do environmental issues affect the other megatrends?

Technological innovations must provide solutions to environmental issues and their consequences. Think of solutions in the field of smart cities and smart mobility, which are environmental-friendly. The possibilities of making work more flexible to counteract the consequences of environmental problems are also being examined: working from home and spreading working hours reduce CO_2 emissions.

There is a clear link between labor migration and environmental issues. Environmental issues can trigger labor migration as extreme weather events, floods, and forest fires force people to look for work elsewhere. This, of course, also has consequences for the labor market and the personnel composition of organizations, both in the areas where employees leave and where they settle. Climate change requires cross-border action and cooperation. Due to increasing globalization, more attention is being paid to an integrated and global approach to environmental issues.

Broadly speaking, there are three categories of solutions to protect the environment:

1. Stop certain activities or start using certain products, and find replacements or new technological solutions.

2. Where technological solutions or substitutes do not exist or are not sufficient, efficiencies should lead to the decoupling of resource use from economic growth.
3. Where stopping certain activities or generating efficiencies is not enough, processes should be fully circular by closing all cycles and eliminating all negative externalities in order to avoid ecological disasters.[11]

In India, 150 million people do not have access to good and safe drinking water. Sarvajal, a technology company in Gujarat, combines old and new technologies to efficiently deliver clean water. UV purification and reverse osmosis filtration units are at the heart of the Sarvajal system, which monitors and adjusts system performance in real time through cloud-based remote monitoring. People can buy water at these water vending machines with a prepaid card. This saves them money because buying water through these vending machines is less expensive than purifying water at home. In addition, the system prevents the waste resulting from individual filtration or large-scale distribution via leaky pipes.[12]

11.6 Self-assessment

How well prepared is your organization for the future when it comes to environmental issues? With these statements from the Futurize! diagnosis (which we discuss in Chapter 18), you can determine for your organization whether it responds well to this megatrend. The statements have been developed by looking at environmental issues from the perspective of the five universal HPO factors. The corresponding HPO factor is given for each statement, and we explain why it is important to aim for a good score for the statement:

- *Management quality: Management shows exemplary behavior in regard to climate reduction.*
  Managers in an HPO work with integrity and are role models for others with their honesty and sincerity. It, therefore, goes without saying that management cannot ask employees to act in an environmentally conscious manner if they themselves do not demonstrate environmentally conscious behavior. By acting as a role model,

management within and outside the organization creates awareness in the field of climate reduction.

- *Openness and action-orientation: The organization is transparent about its ecological footprint and climate reduction initiatives.*

  If an organization is open and honest with regard to its climate impact and improvement initiatives in the field of climate reduction, all stakeholders can contribute ideas and contributions. This can lead to new insights and better initiatives and also contributes to the involvement of employees and stakeholders.

- *Long-term orientation: There is a clear organizational strategy (plan of approach and follow-up) in the field of climate reduction.*

  Organizations are increasingly being asked to demonstrate which goals and initiatives they are taking in the field of climate reduction. A clear strategy for dealing with environmental issues will be indispensable in the near future to qualify as a supplier to environmentally conscious organizations and to attract and retain more and more environmentally conscious employees and customers.

- *Continuous improvement and renewal: The organization works continuously to improve and innovate processes, products, and services with the aim of climate reduction.*

  Not only are improvement and renewal necessary because of the realization that there is only one planet. Organizations will also increasingly have to be able to demonstrate that they are actively working on this theme in order to qualify, for example, as a supplier to environmentally conscious organizations.

- *Employee quality: Employees are actively involved in climate reduction initiatives.*

  The more employees are involved in initiatives, the greater their climate awareness becomes. The chance that they themselves will act in an environmentally conscious way increases, both at work and at home. This is beneficial for climate reduction and for the efficiency of the organization.

According to the International Red Cross's World Disasters Report 2020, there were 24,396 deaths in 2019 from disasters, most of which were related to extreme weather and climate. Non-profit organization Climate Central has calculated that by 2050, 300 million people worldwide will live in areas below sea level, vulnerable to chronic flooding and often without adequate protection. This mainly concerns residents of heavily urbanized areas.[13]

Climate Action 100+, an organization in which 575 large investors are united, has analyzed the policies of 159 large companies and has come to the conclusion that there is no shortage of fine words but that hardly any company is taking enough concrete steps to become climate neutral by 2050. The companies worldwide responsible for 80% of harmful emissions have ambitious targets, but it remains unclear whether they will be achieved and, if so, how.[14]

11.7 How can you prepare?

How can you ensure that your organization is constantly up-to-date and well prepared to respond to increasing environmental issues? Several courses of action emerged from our research:

- Formulate organizational goals with regard to climate reduction and communicate these clearly to the organization and its stakeholders.
- Involve employees in environmental initiatives and translate these into individual contributions from the job or work area.
- Ensure that management (jointly and individually) shows exemplary behavior in the field of CO_2 reduction and other measures against climate change.

Actions by the government, activist groups, and leading profit organizations are increasingly obliging companies to make efforts to solve environmental issues. For instance, investment company Teslin is tightening the climate and social requirements in its portfolio of investments. This way of investing—in which not only return and the shareholder are central but also the impact on the climate and other stakeholders is taken into account—is on the rise. Pension funds and other institutional investors are also increasingly assessing the companies in which they invest against an increasingly strict ESG yardstick (environmental, social, and governance—in other words, ecology, social aspects, and good governance). For example, BNP Paribas no longer finances customers who produce beef or soybeans on farmland that was deforested in the Amazon after 2008, and customers of the bank who buy these products are also no longer financed. In addition, the bank encourages customers not to buy or produce beef or soybeans for which forests in the Cerrado (a savanna area in Brazil) have been cleared or converted to agricultural land after January 1, 2020. BNP Paribas only wants to provide financial products or services to companies with a strategy to eliminate deforestation from their production and supply chains by 2025. Partly under pressure from the government's climate targets, companies are formulating ambitions to reduce CO_2 emissions and use more sustainable energy. Large companies are going green through virtual power deals, and multinationals are increasingly concluding multi-year green power contracts directly with individual wind farms.[15]

Notes

1 United Nations (2019b)
2 Kohlbacher (2017), Kiel et al. (2017), Lamb and Doyle (2017), Peetz (2019)
3 Excerpts from IPCC (2021)
4 Kiel et al. (2017)
5 Bradbury et al. (2021), Luttikhuis (2021)
6 Choi et al. (2019), ILO (2017), Jayne et al. (2017), Lamb and Doyle (2017), Peetz (2019)
7 PWC (2019), Sondermeijer (2021)
8 Bhargava (2020)
9 Noort (2021)
10 Leijten and Tamminga (2021)
11 PWC (2019)
12 Macomber (2013)
13 Aan den Brugh (2021); Kas (2021)
14 Van der Walle (2021)
15 FD (2021b), Kalse (2021b), Van Dijk (2020)

Chapter 12

Economic power shifts

Megatrend 9

12.1 What is it?

Economic power shifts refer to the shift of economic power from the traditional West to the emerging East. Countries in Asia (and to a lesser extent South America and Africa) are growing economically larger and more important due to the growth of their middle class.

The coming decades will be marked by an economic shift to Asia, with investment levels and growth continuing to rise in China, India, and elsewhere. By 2030, 65% of the global middle class will live in Asia (up from 28% in 2009), which is equivalent to 59% of global middle-class consumption. China is expected to surpass the US as the world's largest economy (with its GDP doubling since 2011), followed not far behind by India (with a threefold increase in GDP since 2011). In recent decades, companies in emerging economies have played an increasingly important role at a global level. The lists of the world's most successful companies are no longer completely filled with western names. In fact, today, multinationals from China, India, and Latin America dominate their domestic and international markets.[1]

12.2 Some more explanation

The emerging markets will rewrite the rules of work and work culture as a result of their economic growth, and their political power will increase. This affects the competitive position of organizations in Western countries, making them more vulnerable but at the same time providing growth opportunities in the emerging regions. The growth opportunities will, for example, come from increasing demand in the logistics sector

DOI: 10.4324/9781003273264-12

and the demand for diversity-proof goods and services. The economic power shift will undoubtedly have an impact on the competitive position of organizations in Western countries.

Until fairly recently, the division between developing countries and developed countries (countries that have undergone an industrial revolution and possess or possessed a certain geopolitical power) was relatively clear. But now, the world has changed dramatically: developing countries are moving through industrial changes at lightning speed, often skipping steps in technological revolutions. Currently, the world market consists of traditional developed countries, emerging economies, and multinationals. To continue to believe in an immutable division between developed and developing seems outdated and ignores the major changes caused by technology, innovation, and globalization.[2]

12.3 What are the consequences of economic power shifts for organizations?

The impact of economic power shifts on organizations partly depends on their geographical location and their industry: Western organizations are becoming more vulnerable, and Asian and African companies can benefit from the increased purchasing power in their regions. Organizations looking to expand their business will need to adopt local corporate cultures and practices and hire more diverse employees. At the moment, countries such as India and China offer significant opportunities for organizations that want to grow. The international logistics sector will certainly benefit from this. A risk is that the business environment will become less stable because it is influenced by the political power in those countries.[3]

"We look at the world from a narrow and Western perspective and take it for granted that the West has always been and will remain morally and economically superior. That blinds us to the undeniable fact that most of the new ideas, scientific breakthroughs and innovations used to come from the East. They reached us via the Silk Roads, which linked the higher cultures of Asia and the Middle East with our then dark medieval world. Another, more oriental perspective on the way in which peoples, cultures, trade, politics and continents have always been intertwined shows that East and West share a common world past. Because we in the West have forgotten that, and most politicians and economists still fail to notice, we do to see and understand the logic of the current geopolitical and economic power shift. The center of gravity is gradually shifting back to the East, where it was before the West temporarily gained control of the world and the trade routes."[4]

12.4 What are the opportunities and threats?

According to our research, the megatrend economic powershifts creates opportunities as well as threats for organizations (see Table 12.1).

Table 12.1 The opportunities and threats

Megatrend	Economic power shifts
Opportunities	• The shift to the East means an expansion of the sales market and the size of the labor market (of suitable employees). • The possibilities of selling an organization to a market party from emerging countries are increasing as there is more buying power in emerging countries.
Threats	• Competition is increasing due to the expansion of the market. • The complexity of the organization and its environment is growing. • Internationalization also means that organizations must have knowledge of and comply with local laws and regulations. • The stability of foreign markets, politics, and currencies is less predictable. • Organizations can (still) be unfamiliar with other ways of doing business and, as a result, make cultural mistakes. • Different cultures and groups of employees require different leadership styles.

The Japanese Daiwa House Group takes over Dutch construction company Jan Snel in Montfoort, a specialist in factory production of temporary and permanent housing. Daiwa is already active in Asia, Australia, and North America, is listed on the Tokyo Stock Exchange, and has a turnover of 32 billion. With the takeover, the Japanese are now firmly setting foot on the European market.[5]

12.5 How do economic power shifts influence the other megatrends?

Megatrends and disruptors do not stand alone but can, depending on the situation, strengthen or weaken each other's impact. How do the economic power shifts affect the other megatrends?

Economic power shifts could eventually reduce inequalities as organizations require more workers from diverse backgrounds. They can also trigger a reverse migration: workers remigrate back to their home country because there are more job opportunities there.

12.6 Self-assessment

How well prepared is your organization for the future when it comes to economic power shifts? With these statements from the Futurize! diagnosis (which we discuss in Chapter 18), you can determine for your organization whether it responds well to this megatrend. The statements have been developed by looking at economic power shifts from the perspective of the five universal HPO factors. The corresponding HPO factor is given for each statement, and we explain why it is important to aim for a good score for the statement:

- *Management quality: Management responds and deals well with economic power shifts and geopolitics.*

  By keeping a close eye on the shifts in economic power, the organization can respond in time to new markets or withdraw from certain areas for political reasons, for example.
- *Openness and action-orientation: Opportunities and threats in different countries and markets are monitored and discussed by the organization.*

  By mapping out the developments within different continents and world politics and discussing them within the organization, you increase the insights, and there is a greater chance of acting in a timely manner. This role lies primarily with management, but if you discuss this with employees, surprising ideas for new products, services, or markets can arise.
- *Long-term orientation: There is a clear organizational strategy (plan of action and succession) to respond to economic power shifts and geopolitics.*

  In order to continuously increase the value for the customer, it is important to think ahead, to collaborate with parties in the value chain, and to anticipate the consequences of economic power shifts and geopolitics. This requires a strategy and not an ad hoc approach.

- *Continuous improvement and renewal: When improving and renewing processes, products, and/or services, economic power shifts and geopolitics are taken into account.*

  It is important to test improvements and innovations against possible dependencies or (im)possibilities arising from economic power shifts or geopolitics. This way, your organization will not be surprised by companies, products, or services from emerging markets.

- *Employee quality: Our workforce is a reflection of the international markets in which the organization is (or will become) active.*

  Organizations are likely to do more business with companies from emerging countries and/or customers in those countries. Both require a good intercultural understanding, which an organization must build by hiring employees from different cultural backgrounds, especially from those emerging countries. Their knowledge can also contribute to an improvement of the organizational strategy and tactics with regard to emerging countries.

12.7 How can you prepare?

How can you ensure that your organization is constantly up-to-date and well prepared to respond to economic power shifts? Several courses of action emerged from our research:

- Explore the market and immerse yourself in the culture and the local laws and regulations.
- Hire employees who have knowledge of the culture and ways of working in countries with which you collaborate or where competition can be expected.
- Keep an eye on the plans of the competition from the emerging countries.
- Check for your own organization to what extent it is—or can become—dependent on the consequences of economic power shifts and/or geopolitics.
- Be aware that new markets and new competitors are less predictable.

Notes

1 Pompa (2015)
2 Pompa (2015)
3 Diong (2017), Hajkowicz et al. (2012), Hines (2011), Hoppe et al. (2014)
4 Interview by Jan Willem Velthuijsen, chief economist at PwC, with Peter Frankopan, a professor of world history at the University of Oxford and the author of the books *De zijderoutes: Een nieuwe wereldgeschiedenis* (*The Silk Roads: A New World History*, 2015) and *De nieuwe zijderoutes: Het heden en de toekomst van de wereld* (*The New Silk Roads: The Present and Future of the World*, 2018).
5 Cobouw (2020)

Chapter 13

Urbanization
Megatrend 10

13.1 What is it?

Megatrend urbanization refers to the worldwide migration of the population from rural to urban areas. As a result, an increasing number of people are permanently concentrated in relatively small areas (cities or metropolitan areas).

It is expected that 80% of the population growth in Africa in the coming decades will take place in the cities, which means that this continent will experience the highest degree of urbanization in the world. By 2030, there will be seventeen African cities with more than five million inhabitants, with Cairo, Lagos, Kinshasa, Luanda, and Dar es Salaam growing to a population of more than ten million inhabitants. By 2037, the majority of the African population will live in cities. But in the Western world, urbanization is also still going on. For example, forecasts by the United Nations show that in 2050 the urbanization rate in the already densely populated areas in the Netherlands will be 96% (currently 90%). Nearly all inhabitants of the Netherlands will then live in a city. The reasons for the march toward the city are diverse but the same all over the world: better career prospects, attractiveness of the facilities, and the social and cultural offers within a city. The rapid growth of cities creates an increasing demand there for products and services, such as infrastructure, retail, banking, agriculture, and commodities.[1]

13.2 Some more explanation

Urbanization has implications for organizations in both rural and urban areas. In rural areas, there can be a shortage of qualified workers, leading to organizational problems. On the contrary, urban areas are becoming too crowded, resulting in higher living costs, competition for jobs, and a more

DOI: 10.4324/9781003273264-13

hectic/unbalanced life and resulting health problems. On the other hand, urbanization offers opportunities for both skilled (e.g., business services) and unskilled workers (e.g., construction and housing). In Asia and Africa in particular, urbanization can enhance competitiveness if properly managed. Various sources warn, though, that insufficient attention to financing and management of cities can lead to major social and economic problems.[2]

13.3 What are the consequences of urbanization for organizations?

Urbanization leads to a brain drain from rural areas to cities. This creates a shortage of qualified employees in rural areas. Organizations in these regions will have to invest extra to attract suitable employees or also have to move to urban areas themselves. Organizations in urban areas can benefit from the increasing demand for their products and services if resources, transport, and mobility are properly managed.

13.4 What are the opportunities and threats?

According to our research, the megatrend urbanization creates opportunities as well as threats for organizations (see Table 13.1).

Table 13.1 The opportunities and threats

Megatrend	Urbanization
Opportunities	• Organizations in urban areas will have a growing workforce at their disposal. • Organizations targeting urban areas see a growing market for their products and services.
Threats	• There will be a shortage of suitable employees in non-urban areas (brain drain). • The cost of living in urban areas will increase further. • The organization needs to change its ways of providing services because of more (and possibly different types of) stakeholders arising from urbanization. • Urbanization can have a negative impact on healthy living conditions in urban areas.

Every country in the world has needed urbanization to boost productivity gains that lead to higher incomes. However, urban areas face a paradox: they concentrate wealth and employment but at the same time suffer from poverty and exclusion. A form of exclusion occurs in the labor market. As land prices rise—driven by the city's success in attracting businesses and workers—housing becomes less affordable. Poorer workers and members of vulnerable groups are settling in dangerous, poorly connected, and poorly maintained urban areas further away from their jobs. Such a spatial mismatch between residence and job can be seen in cities from Chicago to Johannesburg. As a result, cities are places where wealth and poverty coexist and where opportunity and exclusion coexist.[3]

13.5 How does urbanization influence the other megatrends?

Megatrends and disruptors do not stand alone but can, depending on the situation, strengthen or weaken each other's impact. How does urbanization affect the other megatrends?

Flexible work, especially via platforms, can counter the trend of urbanization, as people from rural areas have their jobs in the city but continue to live in the countryside. With an increase in flex workers, there is a chance that they will receive less management attention as a group, resulting in a less engaged workforce with lower quality and motivation. Especially in combination with older employees and employees with special needs that require more attention from management, this can result in an increase in diversity of the workforce.

Urbanization is already leading to an increase in the power of regions in developing countries (economic power shifts). But if not managed properly, urbanization can become the Achilles heel of developing countries for lack of resources, such as water and reliable energy supply.

Cities around the world are experiencing the effects of various megatrends that create opportunities and challenges. First, demographic changes are driving an aging population in developed countries and a growing urban population in developing countries. Aging implies a declining labor supply and an increasing demand for health and personal care jobs; these jobs are an opportunity for migrants from developing countries. In developing countries, urbanization implies the need for infrastructure to anticipate urban population growth. Expanding basic urban infrastructure (such as water, sanitation, and transport) is not only essential to maintain and improve the well-being of urban residents but is also a source of employment. Cities create jobs if they succeed in attracting both businesses and workers. Businesses are attracted to cities by the benefits they derive from sharing knowledge and infrastructure with other businesses and matching interests with those of employees, suppliers, and customers. The Danish Kalundborg, for example, has the world's first center for industrial symbiosis. Companies in this cluster exchange waste and by-products to reduce costs and CO_2 emissions, and the collaboration ensures that all participants benefit from the exchange of knowledge, materials, information, and resources. Finally, workers are attracted to cities by higher wages, a wider variety of jobs, and consumption options.[4]

13.6 Self-assessment

How well prepared is your organization for the future when it comes to urbanization? With these statements from the Futurize! diagnosis (which we discuss in Chapter 18), you can determine for your organization whether it responds well to this megatrend. The statements have been developed by looking at urbanization from the perspective of the five universal HPO factors. The corresponding HPO factor is given for each statement, and we explain why it is important to aim for a good score for the statement:

- *Management quality: The organization pays a lot of attention to the working conditions of both its urban and rural employees.*

    By paying attention to the working conditions of the employees, the organization is able to retain them. Depending on the location of both the organization and the employee, this means, for example, investing in accessibility, parking spaces, home workplaces, and communication facilities.

- *Openness and action-orientation: The organization investigates the consequences of urbanization on the organization and its customers and employees and then responds accordingly.*

    It makes sense for an organization to delve into the needs of customers in specific areas. By responding to this in the right way, it can distinguish itself from the competition. In addition to adapting specific products or services, this also includes sponsoring local initiatives to increase visibility. The consequences of urbanization on employees must also be mapped out, by discussing this with them, for example, so that the organization can meet the mobility and working-from-home wishes of employees.

- *Long-term orientation: There is a clear organizational strategy (plan of approach and follow-up) to respond to urbanization.*

With a good urbanization strategy, the organization can respond to, for example, accessibility (transport), specific needs within both urban and rural areas, and the availability of sufficient personnel. In this way, the organization can make urbanization work to its advantage.

- *Continuous improvement and renewal: Processes, products, and/ or services are continuously improved and renewed to respond to urbanization.*

  It is important to continuously improve and innovate in order to remain competitive/distinctive in relation to competitors. When dealing with the consequences of urbanization, organizational development will have to focus on transport and the specific needs of the rural or urban environment. With regard to the internal organization, extra investment must be made in recruiting and retaining high-quality employees.

- *Employee quality: The organization ensures sufficient growth of high-quality employees in the immediate vicinity of the location.*

  Wherever an organization is located, it is always good to keep commuting to a minimum as it often entails unnecessary travel time (negative effect on the work-life balance) and burdens the environment. An organization would, therefore, do well to create a connection with the society within its location region. But sometimes this is not possible because the necessary employees are not available in the immediate vicinity. In that case, investments can be made in options for flexible working and, on the other hand, in training staff in the area by collaborating with local training institutes, for example.

The quality of urban life is becoming increasingly important for attracting dynamic companies and qualified employees. In developing countries, cities must provide the basic infrastructure (water, sewage, public transport) to enable that growth. They also have the ability to plan urbanization to reduce congestion costs, facilitate housing construction, improve amenities, and create jobs. New building technologies and materials can reduce energy consumption. By harnessing unused land and easing restrictions on land markets, they can also improve housing affordability. In developed countries, livability in cities can be improved by addressing some of the negative externalities of agglomerations, such as pollution. Local approaches, such as more compact cities that reduce travel time and CO_2 emissions, can increase livability and better address the challenges of sustainability.[5]

13.7 How can you prepare?

How can you ensure that your organization is constantly up-to-date and well prepared to respond to increasing urbanization? Several courses of action emerged from our research:

- Motivate employees to live and work outside urban areas (for example, by offering parking spaces or a public transport subscription at hard-to-reach rural work locations, by arranging home working facilities and flexible working hours to avoid traffic jams, by offering childcare and various services such as dry cleaning or takeaway at work, and by renting satellite office space).
- Ensure brand awareness and loyalty by sponsoring local (sports) clubs and neighborhood associations.
- Offer work and training places, especially for regional training. This helps to attract and retain employees from the region.
- Support local entrepreneurs by purchasing from local organizations (fruit at work, flowers). This promotes stakeholder loyalty.
- Form a local community by contributing to a good cause (for example, the food bank).
- Offer careers in collaboration with an industrial circle.

Notes

1 Menkveld (2016, 2019), VNO-NCW en MKB-Nederland (2019)
2 Biswas et al. (2018), Diong (2017), Hajkowicz et al. (2012), Malik and Janowska (2018), National Intelligence Council (2012), Retief et al. (2016)
3 Sanchez-Reaza et al. (2018)
4 Sanchez-Reaza et al. (2018), PWC (2019)
5 Sanchez-Reaza et al. (2018)

Chapter 14

Cross-border migration
Megatrend 11

14.1 What is it?

Cross-border migration refers to the migration of workers, usually from their home country, to another country with the aim of finding (better) work. Cross-border migration arises in a world where people in their country of origin do not find attractive employment opportunities, while other economies cannot sufficiently fill their staff shortages.

> In an increasingly connected global market, cross-border migration plays a major role. The best-skilled workers cross borders to earn the best salaries, while low-skilled workers are limited in their ability to migrate. Many students from the developing world find their way to the best universities and schools in the world. Some of them return to their home countries as highly skilled workers, while others stay where they were educated, adding to the economic strength of the host country. In those countries where certain sectors have a high demand for skilled workers, foreign youth may be able to receive training to meet that demand. Conversely, young people with skills needed abroad are better able to find jobs across borders. Indeed, many countries with serious skills shortages will need to review their migration policies.[1]

14.2 Some more explanation

Cross-border migration changes the composition of the workforce and can cause social problems. Migrants are more vulnerable than native workers, and unemployment among them is higher, especially if they have a non-Western background.[2] The increase in migration is changing the composition of the labor force in "receiving countries," while at the same time, this "leaving" knowledge and skills are badly needed in the countries of origin of the migrants (countries with low wages, subject

DOI: 10.4324/9781003273264-14

to climate change, politically unstable). There are also mutual migration flows. In Amsterdam, for example, Romanian workers work in low-paid and unskilled jobs, while the resulting vacancies in Romania are in turn filled by Ukrainians, among others. This kind of economic immigration—with workers far away from their friends and family, housed in small, expensive rooms in cities—is hardly sustainable. Organizations need to prepare for a more diverse workforce (in culture, religion, and language) while at the same time becoming more aware of the effects of migration on sustainable value creation.

> Language problems and different ways of communicating often lead to misunderstandings. If a manager asks a status holder to do something, he will quickly nod yes, even if he does not actually understand the assignment. Discrimination also occurs, especially in a workplace where few people with different cultural background work.[3]

14.3 What are the consequences of cross-border migration for organizations?

Organizations can fill workforce gaps in numbers and skills with migrant workers. Cross-border migration changes the composition of the workforce in both the immigrant's country of origin and the host country. For organizations in the country of origin, this means an exodus of knowledge and skills. These organizations have to look for new employees, and this can again be migrant employees from other countries. In the receiving countries—due to miscommunication (different languages) and cultural differences—an increase in the number of employees from different cultural backgrounds can lead to tensions and social problems in an organization. Organizations will then have to invest in, for example, culture programs.[4]

14.4 What are the opportunities and threats?

According to our research, the megatrend cross-border migration creates opportunities as well as threats for organizations (see Table 14.1).

Table 14.1 The opportunities and threats

Megatrend	Cross-border migration
Opportunities	• Dealing properly (decently) with labor migrants can strengthen trust in the organization. • Hiring migrant workers can fill a labor shortage. • Working with different cultures can improve current products and services and yield new products and services due to the increased diversity in the organization.

Megatrend	Cross-border migration
Threats	• Stress and suboptimal living conditions can have negative consequences for the health of migrant workers. This is detrimental not only to the people involved but also to their productivity in the organization. • Organizations must invest (extra) in training and sustainable employability of labor migrants. • Integration and guidance of labor migrants require extra attention. • The fact that people come from different cultures makes communication, knowledge exchange, and performance orientation difficult because they might not understand each other well. • Workers with special needs—in this case, migrant workers—require more attention from management and new ways and processes to meet these needs.

Many developing countries, currently especially in Central and South America, are struggling to keep highly skilled young people in the country. The best and brightest people from developing countries migrate to countries that offer greater economic benefits, leaving the home country without highly skilled workers. The percentage of brain drain for these regions has only increased in recent decades, leaving many companies in these regions looking for qualified employees experiencing stress and difficulties.[5]

14.5 How does cross-border migration influence the other megatrends?

Megatrends and disruptors do not stand alone but can, depending on the situation, strengthen or weaken each other's impact. How does cross-border migration affect the other megatrends?

Immigrated workers can be a solution to the labor shortage in the host country, but also the cause of a labor shortage in countries where people choose to leave. This can have a major impact on the composition of the workforce in organizations in both the receiving country and the departing country. Migrant workers and specific groups of workers are also more vulnerable. Because they are away from their own culture, family, and friends (increasing inequality), they enjoy less (social) protection and experience more stress.

Asia also sees a shift in migration patterns, especially within the highly educated workforce. Attractive employment opportunities in Asia are increasing, and higher wages are being paid. As a result, there are more opportunities domestically than abroad, and more and more highly skilled workers will stay in (or return to) the region instead of going abroad as before. As Asia is one of the most important regions for human capital exports, it is bringing about major changes in current demographic patterns, information and technology flows, and geopolitics. Couple this with the fact that education levels are rising across the spectrum in Asia, and it becomes clear that the coming decades will look fundamentally different from today.[6] In the same token, cross-border migration has also taken hold in the South African region. The economic buoyancy of countries like South Africa and Botswana has attracted thousands of migrants in the region who are seeking job opportunities, straining government resources and impeding the effective functioning of border immigration services. In addition, the unequal rate of economic development in the region has created an increasing gap between fast-developing and slow-developing nations, causing an unequal rate of migration. Skills transfer and collaborations have been the major benefits of cross-border migration for SADC, although crime and xenophobia have also been identified as problems associated with cross-border migration in South Africa.[7]

14.6 Self-assessment

How well prepared is your organization for the future when it comes to cross-border migration? With these statements from the Futurize! diagnosis (which we discuss in Chapter 18), you can determine for your organization whether it responds well to this megatrend. The statements have been developed by looking at cross-border migration from the perspective of the five universal HPO factors. The corresponding HPO factor is given for each statement, and we explain why it is important to aim for a good score for the statement:

- *Management quality: Management treats migrant workers with the same respect (safety, health, security) like other employees.*
  When management acts as a role model in a hospitable and open-minded manner toward labor migrants and thus shows that all employees are treated equally and fairly, this behavior is considered normal, and labor migrants will quickly feel at home in the organization.
- *Openness and action-orientation: The organization is open about the opportunities and threats of labor migration.*

Cross-border migration can certainly offer a solution, but it also presents a number of challenges, due to differences in communication and culture, for example. It is important to face and address these challenges, be open about both the benefits and challenges of hiring migrant workers in the organization, and talk about this with all employees. Then the labor migrants are more easily integrated into the organization, and they can function optimally, quicker.

- *Long-term orientation: There is a clear organizational strategy (plan of approach and follow-up) to respond to and deal with cross-border migration.*

    In order to respond effectively to cross-border migration, it is important to map out the expected migration movements and to develop a plan for making provisions for the different types of employees, which can be expected to arrive. Successful implementation of this requires the attention and time of the entire organization.

- *Continuous improvement and renewal: The organization tries to combat cross-border migration by paying fair wages and providing good working conditions in all countries it operates.*

    In an ideal world, people can carry out their work in the environment where they live. It is important here that organizations in the home countries of the potential labor migrants have subsidiaries where good and decent working conditions prevail. The head office of those organizations must then regularly check whether good employment conditions are actually offered locally.

- *Employee quality: The organization offers sustainable working conditions (with decent working hours, working conditions, and training) to all employees, regardless of where they come from.*

    Healthy and well-trained migrant workers contribute to the success of the organization. That is why it is important to pay attention to sustainable employment terms (and conditions), regardless of the location where employees are working.

14.7 How can you prepare?

How can you ensure that your organization is constantly up-to-date and well prepared to respond to increasing cross-border migration? Several courses of action emerged from our research:

- Invest in education and training programs for migrant workers in the receiving countries.
- Offer good working conditions in all countries and regions where the organization is located so that people do not have to move because of the opportunity for better work or pay elsewhere.

- Invest in culture programs within the organization to prevent miscommunication and misunderstanding between different groups of employees.

Notes

1 Pompa (2015)
2 De Lange (2019), Woetzel et al. (2016)
3 Toe Laer (2021)
4 Kaivo-Oja et al. (2017), Manyika et al. (2017), Woetzel et al. (2016), World Bank (2019), World Economic Forum (2018b)
5 Pompa (2015)
6 Pompa (2015)
7 Mlambo (2018)

Chapter 15

Resource scarcity
Megatrend 12

15.1 What is it?

The ever-increasing global demand for resources (such as water, food, energy, land, and minerals) causes scarcity and inherent increases in costs.

15.2 Some more explanation

Global consumption has increased dramatically over the past century, impacting the demand for and use of natural resources and raw materials.[1] Organizations increasingly need to rethink and tackle their dependence on scarce raw materials and resources. Finding new ways of working, innovating, and using alternative means is the key for organizations to survive in the future. If leaders do not respond to this based on intrinsic motivation, society will force them to minimize the negative effects of their organization on society and the environment. Fossil fuels are finite and must be replaced in the short term by alternatives such as wind and solar energy. The increasing water shortage is a major problem as water is used in many production processes, including food production.[2]

Since the 1970s, there has been an ecological deficit in terms of environmental impact. This means that the global annual demand for resources is about 75% greater than what the earth can regenerate each year. Today, the global economy uses the equivalent of 1.7 planets for global waste production and processing. A good method for measuring the impact of human activity on nature is the global footprint. It quantifies the pressure that human economic activity exerts on nature through a supply-and-demand methodology. Here, supply is that which nature can regenerate in a certain period, and demand consists of the resources that human activities require during the same period, measured in a certain

DOI: 10.4324/9781003273264-15

geographical area. An ecological deficit occurs when consumption by a population of people exceeds the biocapacity of the area available for that population. A national ecological deficit means that a nation exports biocapacity through trade, consumes its national ecological assets, and releases CO_2 into the atmosphere. An ecological reserve exists when the biocapacity of an area exceeds the consumption needs of the population.[3]

15.3 What are the consequences of resource scarcity for organizations?

The increasing scarcity of raw materials hinders production processes and drives up the cost price of products. The prices of raw materials and consumer goods will rise and/or the quality of the products will fall. Especially for production processes with intensive water consumption, new production methods have to be found. The increasing scarcity demands (even) more attention from the next generations for the risks of overconsumption and waste. More legislation will be introduced from the government on the regulated use of resources, and tax rates for specific sources are expected to increase in certain countries.

15.4 What are the opportunities and threats?

According to our research, the megatrend resource scarcity creates opportunities as well as threats for organizations (see Table 15.1).

Table 15.1 The opportunities and threats

Megatrend	Resource scarcity
Opportunities	• The general trend of sustainable employment practices and attention to environmental issues, and reduction of raw material consumption can strengthen the trust of customers, stakeholders, and employees in the organization. • Scarcity forces innovation. • A work environment that explicitly takes into account the consumption of raw materials will attract and retain stakeholders and employees who find this important.
Threats	• Lack of raw materials leads to production problems and cost increases. • Management should spend much more time dealing with resource scarcity. • Resource scarcity requires a lot of dialogue time and process improvement capacity. • The organization has to establish closer ties with suppliers to survive times of scarcity. • Strategy and processes are adversely affected in times of scarce resources.

Conflict minerals are minerals that are in high demand and are scarce on the global market. The proceeds are (possibly) used to fund armed groups, incite forced labor and other human rights abuses, and support corruption and money laundering. These conflict minerals include tin, tungsten, tantalum, and gold. They are won in countries and regions that suffer from armed conflict, such as a civil war, or are weakened after a regional conflict.[4]

15.5 How does resource scarcity influence the other megatrends?

Megatrends and disruptors do not stand alone but can, depending on the situation, strengthen or weaken each other's impact. How does resource scarcity affect the other megatrends?

When looking for solutions to the scarcity of resources, it is imperative to look for alternatives to raw materials and for new production methods. Technological progress can play a major role in this. A concrete solution for reducing the use of fossil fuels can be sought in the area of flexible employment (more working from home). The scarcity of raw materials has a strong relationship with environmental issues. The extraction of raw materials from the earth, by cutting down tropical rainforests, for example, has led to far-reaching consequences for nature and biodiversity.

Thanks to the use of natural resources and the reduction of waste, a good sustainability strategy can improve operational efficiency and thus save costs. See, for example, Nestlé's sustainability strategy, which focuses on water conservation. At the company's manufacturing operations in drought-prone South Africa, improvements in wastewater reduction and water recovery over a five-year period have increased factory production by 32% while reducing water and water management costs by 12%.[5]

15.6 Self-assessment

How well prepared is your organization for the future when it comes to resource scarcity? With these statements from the Futurize! diagnosis (which we discuss in Chapter 18), you can determine for your organization whether it responds well to this megatrend. The statements have been developed by looking at resource scarcity from the perspective of the five universal HPO factors. The corresponding HPO factor is given for each statement, and we explain why it is important to aim for a good score for the statement:

- *Management quality: Management takes the lead in reducing its personal ecological footprint.*

    Managers in an HPO act with integrity and are role models for employees and stakeholders of the organization in regard to using scarce resources. In this way, they encourage employees to think about and contribute to reducing the ecological footprint of the organization and themselves.

- *Openness and action-orientation: The organization keeps track of its consumption of scarce raw materials and reports this regularly to the stakeholders.*

    Organizations increasingly need to be able to demonstrate that they work in a sustainable way and are looking for alternative solutions for the use of scarce raw materials. An example in this regard is tracking and reporting the use of scarce raw materials. Suppliers, customers, and employees are increasingly opting for organizations that are consciously involved in this.

- *Long-term orientation: There is a clear organizational strategy (plan of approach and follow-up) to become less dependent on scarce raw materials.*

    Resource scarcity is an ongoing problem that organizations and their partners in the value chain must take into account. Organizations have to look for new solutions for production processes and alternative raw materials. This often has far-reaching consequences for the processes and the logistics chain. Dealing with this problem requires a clear strategy.

- *Continuous improvement and renewal: The organization continuously adapts its processes and products so that they require less or no scarce raw materials.*

    An organization can reduce the use of scarce raw materials with the help of innovation. This makes it less dependent on these raw materials. This has positive consequences not only for the ecological footprint but also for the image of the organization.

- *Employee quality: Employees are consciously engaged in reducing the use of scarce raw materials.*

    It is important that not only management but also employees are aware of the need to reduce the consumption of scarce raw materials. Everyone must have sufficient knowledge to be able to anticipate and act on this in their daily work. It is the responsibility of management to inform and motivate employees to reduce the use of scarce raw materials on the one hand and to think about alternatives on the other.

The scarcity of raw materials is one of the reasons why Danone now prefers biobased plastics to plastics produced from fossil raw materials for the packaging of its dairy products. Apple wants to end its dependence on minerals by using only recycled materials, such as aluminum, copper, tin, and tungsten, in its devices. In addition to scarcity, risk factors with regard to the supply of these materials also play a role in the ambition of the company (such as the big companies buying up all these materials at the expense of smaller organizations). The company Bio-lutions has developed a patented process to make disposable tableware and packaging from agricultural waste. Those residues are converted into self-binding fibers that require no additives or chemicals, after which they are shaped and pressed to make the crockery and packaging. The products can be returned to the natural cycle by composting or recycled after use. Adidas's Futurecraft.Loop project has developed a fully recyclable running shoe, made from one material and without the use of glue. When the shoes are discarded, the material is cleaned, pelletized, and melted down into a material that can be used to make a new pair of shoes. Werner & Mertz, a manufacturer of laundry, care, and cleaning products, cofounded the Recyclat initiative with a number of other companies. Thanks to this project, 80% of recycled materials can be used in PET packaging, collected from standard household waste. Werner & Mertz now focuses on packaging that is fully recyclable and made from a single material, making it more suitable for sorting and processing.[6]

15.7 How can you prepare?

How can you ensure that your organization is constantly up-to-date and well prepared to respond to the increasing resource scarcity? Several courses of action emerged from our research:

- As an organization, offer room for innovation through experiments, research, and development. Organize challenges, dialogues, and brainstorming sessions.

- Involve employees with interest in sustainable solutions. Younger generations often bring new insights, especially in the field of sustainability.
- Enter into a partnership with a training institute (teaching, internship, research position) to gain new knowledge together.

Notes

1 Diong (2017), Retief et al. (2016)
2 Esposito and Tse (2018)
3 PWC (2019)
4 PWC (2019)
5 Whelan and Douglas (2021)
6 PWC (2019)

Chapter 16

Individualism
Megatrend 13

16.1 What is it?

Individualism refers to the trend to distinguish oneself from another as a person and individual. This trend is a result of a shift from a collectivist society to a focus on the individual and the increasing expectations of those individuals regarding the availability of goods and services tailored to their specific needs at the time they wish.

16.2 Some more explanation

People and organizations increasingly expect tailor-made and personalized products, services, and solutions. This development is driving the pace of societies towards 24-hour services, which is made possible by the ubiquity of ICT and the expansion of e-commerce, e-shopping, and mobile services.[1] Organizations must respond to the increasing demand for individual attention. Customer experience and employee experience are important performance indicators today, and these have to be closely monitored. As a result, more and more personalized products and services are offered, such as personalized education.[2] Instead of generic training programs, universities are increasingly developing individualized training. The same applies to corporate training, which is increasingly tailored to individual career aspirations.

Here are a number of examples of increasing individualism:[3]

- The central role of marriage continues to crumble: younger generations increasingly live together unmarried, more children are born out of wedlock, the percentage of divorced people continues to rise, and there are more and more single-person households.

DOI: 10.4324/9781003273264-16

- Traditional social ties are becoming less important: there is a strong decrease in people who are ecclesiastical, and there is a gradual decline in trade union membership (while, for that matter, the membership of idealistic organizations remains stable).
- People are becoming unique and more independent: children's names are more often unique, and the time when the man was the (primary) breadwinner in the household is over.
- Social and societal participation is not less but different: there is a growth in social contacts via the Internet, and more relationships are created via the Internet, while at the same time, the social isolation of (certain groups of) people is increasing.

16.3 What are the consequences of individualism for organizations?

Individualism leads to increasing demand for 24/7 availability, specialization, and personalization of goods and services. Customer experience plays a greater role than ever, and organizations must increasingly respond to the individual wishes of those customers. This requires a new way of looking at the market and perhaps even new production processes. Employees also expect more customization from their employers in their terms and conditions of employment. Organizations will have to adapt to this if they are to be able to attract and retain qualified personnel.

16.4 What are the opportunities and threats?

According to our research, the megatrend individualism creates opportunities as well as threats for organizations, (see Table 16.1).

Table 16.1 The opportunities and threats

Megatrend	Individualism
Opportunities	• There is extra turnover through personalized products and services.
Threats	• Management must make more effort to respond to the different needs, wishes, and views of employees.
	• Assembly line production processes increasingly need to be converted to smaller runs and customization.
	• Marketing to customer groups is becoming less relevant and effective.

More and more companies are responding to the trend of individualism. Facebook filters your contacts based on the number of links you click: if you often click on certain people's links, they will come to the top, while the people you click on little will slowly "sink." Nike is strongly committed to customization: designing your own clothes, shoes, and accessories. There is the Nike ID, for example, where you design your shoes yourself by choosing the colors, the material of certain parts, and the sole. The G-Star RAW Tailored Atelier is a traveling studio where you can have your trousers assembled by hand on the spot. You choose your buttons, material, and label yourself, and one-of-a-kind denim pants are created for you.[4]

16.5 How does individualism influence the other megatrends?

Megatrends and disruptors do not stand alone but can, depending on the situation, strengthen or weaken each other's impact. How does individualism affect the other megatrends?

Increasing individualism requires technological innovations to be able to quickly offer personalized and specialized solutions. Thanks to the 24-hour economy and e-commerce, customers can go anywhere in the world at any time for their ideal product or service (globalization). The increasing demand for the continuous availability of organizations and infrastructures can also lead to energy scarcity in the long run (environmental issues).

Individualism at the work level can lead to more flexible work and more sustainable work through, for example, a better work-life balance and remote working. With this, the focus on the individual supports the diverse preferences of generations and employees. Individualism in relation to economic power shifts leads to potential growth in demand in developing countries and for organizations that want to play a role in those developing countries.

With the IKEA app on your smartphone, it is possible to scan your living room, which gives you a digital version, including all furniture in the correct dimensions. You can choose a new piece of furniture in the digital IKEA catalog. Then place it directly in your digital living room to see if it fits, looks good, and matches your personal taste and style. If so, you can order and pay for that piece of furniture immediately, after which it will be delivered to your home the next day. And if you need help putting together your purchase, the app will give you step-by-step instructions for this.[5]

16.6 Self-assessment

How well prepared is your organization for the future when it comes to increased individualism? With these statements from the Futurize! diagnosis (which we discuss in Chapter 18), you can determine for your organization whether it responds well to this megatrend. The statements have been developed by looking at individualism from the perspective of the five universal HPO factors. The corresponding HPO factor is given for each statement, and we explain why it is important to aim for a good score for the statement:

- *Management quality: Management shows genuine interest in individual employees.*
  In an individualistic society, employees want to receive personal recognition and appreciation. It is important that managers are aware of this and respond to this by, for example, having one-on-one conversations with employees, giving them compliments, and offering them opportunities to develop individually (and not always in groups).
- *Openness and action-orientation: The organization investigates the individual wishes and motivations of employees and takes these into account as much as possible.*
  In order to be able to respond to the individual needs of employees (and customers), it is important to know what these needs are. Periodic employee surveys can contribute to this, as long as the organization does not forget to follow up on the survey results.
- *Long-term orientation: There is a clear strategy (plan of approach and follow-up) to respond to increasing individualism.*
  A clear strategy is necessary in order to permanently bind employees and customers to the organization. The organization must decide how far it will go with meeting the diverse needs of customers and employees. To what level is the organization able and/or willing to personalize products or services or to meet the individual requirements

of employees? To determine a good strategy, the organization must, of course, first map out customer and employee needs.

- *Continuous improvement and renewal: Processes are made flexible in such a way that they deliver products and services that meet the individual wishes and requirements of the customers.*

  Flexibility is paramount when renewing and improving programs and processes so that customization can be achieved quickly. In this way, different individual customer needs can be met as much as possible.

- *Employee quality: Training, coaching, and appreciation programs are personalized (tailored to the needs of the individual employee).*

  Employees expect more and more individual freedom of choice in terms of employment and training opportunities and are more likely to choose organizations that provide these. Offering standard conditions and programs for training and guidance no longer meets the needs of employees. The organization must respond to individual demands in order to be able to find or retain suitable employees in the long term.

Individualism in society affects the relationship between employer and employee. Employees like to see that their employer matches their wishes. However, employers appear to find it difficult to create a good work-life balance for their employees, while this is becoming increasingly important, especially for young generations. An important reason for this is that many companies are still trying to put employees in molds, even though the employment relationship between employer and employee is no longer based on unambiguous laws and rules that are roughly the same for everyone.[6]

16.7 How can you prepare?

How can you ensure that your organization is constantly up-to-date and well prepared to respond to increasing individualism? Several courses of action emerged from our research:

- Make sure that the organization knows what employees find important by, for example, means of regular employee surveys.
- Make sure that the organization knows what the customers find important with the use of regular customer surveys, for example.

- Structure improvement and development initiatives in such a way that different target groups and generations of employees can get involved so that everyone gets a chance.
- Involve different target groups of employees in projects to benefit from as many different insights and ideas as possible.
- Offer freedom of choice regarding training and development, career paths, and flexible working conditions (e.g., a personal budget). Let employees develop their own set of tasks (job crafting).

Notes

1 Tinnilä (2012), Von der Gracht and Darkow (2010)
2 Hessel (2014)
3 CBS (2017)
4 Trends website (2021), Concept Design (Nl), https://trendsnl.wordpress.com/2013/02/11/je-eigen-gefilterde-wereldje/
5 Diamandis and Kotler (2020)
6 CompanyMatch (2016)

Chapter 17

Pandemics

Disruptor 1

17.1 What is it?

Pandemics place extraordinary demands on public health and medical care and threaten the functioning and even survival of organizations. Major outbreaks have serious, often long-lasting effects on business and society as a whole. The economic and fiscal aftermath—in the form of severe shocks to investment, production, and consumption—will often last longer than the epidemiological consequences themselves.

> "Viruses remain and the world must adapt to future virus outbreaks. Therefore, there is no time before or after corona. For the longer term, more strategies must be in place and all countries must have virus adaptation policies."[1]

17.2 Some more explanation

Interestingly enough, we found only one disruptor mentioned in relation to the literature related to the "future of work": the occurrence of a pandemic. Other possible disruptors—such as (nuclear) war (especially on a large scale), regional conflicts with global consequences (such as a war with Iran), infrastructural disasters (caused by, for example, foreign hackers), collapse of economic power blocs (such as the EU or China), or natural phenomena (such as solar geomagnetic storms)—are discussed (here and there) in the literature but not specifically their implications for the future of work. The pandemic disruptor itself was also mentioned only six times in the literature consulted. This is remarkable because, for example, in recent decades, every US president has had to respond to at least one pandemic.[2] As a side effect of globalization and because

DOI: 10.4324/9781003273264-17

of the increasing risk of infectious diseases related to climate change, this will only increase. In addition, an outbreak of, say, a flu pandemic could be more disastrous than a nuclear exchange between two belligerent nations.[3]

In general, current systems, procedures, and capabilities to adequately manage the outbreak of pandemics are not sufficient to cope with the rapid spread and the shocking effects on health, social, and economic systems. The consequences of a pandemic can, therefore, be extremely serious for individual organizations and the business community and society as a whole.[4]

According to a McKinsey Global Institute study of the post-pandemic economy, the lasting effects of COVID-19 on the future of work are expected to be as follows:

- The physical dimension of work is now an important new factor shaping the future of work due to health and safety considerations. This is especially true for work, with a high degree of physical proximity: leisure and travel locations (including restaurants and hotels), on-site customer interaction (including retail and hospitality), office work using computers, and manufacturing and warehousing. In work areas with less physical proximity, such as outdoor work, the effects of the pandemic are expected to fade quickly. Fields of work, such as medical care and personal care, with traditionally a high degree of physical proximity, will also show less change because physical precautions have always been taken there.
- Hybrid working (alternating home and work location) is expected to continue: up to 25% of workers in advanced economies and 10% in emerging economies could continue to work from home three to five days a week. That is four to five times more than before the pandemic. The demand for public transport, restaurants, and shops in urban centers will decrease as a result.
- The growth of the share of e-commerce and the delivery economy (e.g., home delivery) continues. This will permanently reduce the number of jobs in brick-and-mortar stores and restaurants, while employment in distribution centers and last-mile delivery increases.
- Organizations have mostly applied automation and AI to cope with COVID-19 disruptions. In the coming years, they will do this to a greater extent by placing more robots in factories and

warehouses, installing self-service kiosks for customers, and using service robots for customer interactions.

- Major cities will feel the impact of these developments as working from home reduces the demand for retail and food service. Smaller cities, where these facilities declined before the pandemic, can actually benefit from this.
- A large part of the current working population will have to change occupations by 2030. Workers without university degrees, ethnic minorities, and young people are most affected in this regard.

17.3 What are the consequences of pandemics for organizations?

With regard to the recent corona epidemic, we can name several consequences. Complex and failing global supply chains have been shown to have a major detrimental impact on the health sector. The global integration of industries and businesses has created a (too) high degree of vulnerability.[5] The corona crisis will undoubtedly have a negative effect on the future free movement of people and goods across borders, thus reviving local industries. The use of digital communication tools and advanced technologies, such as 3D printing, digital solutions, digital currencies, and AI, has increased dramatically during the crisis. The question is, what will be the implications for more traditional companies and industries in the longer term? Pandemics are impacting the health of staff and the way organizations work, leading to the accelerated adoption of digitization and home working. Face-to-face meetings are being replaced by online meetings. These new ways of working will continue after the crisis; the question is to what degree.

When it comes to severe economic downturns and recessions (caused by a pandemic), history shows two developments. First, there are companies that profit. During the last four economic crises, several large companies have increased both their revenue growth and their EBIT (earnings before interest and tax) margin by 14%. Second, crises lead not only to temporary but also to permanent changes. The terrorist attacks of 9/11, for example, caused only a temporary decrease in air travel but a permanent shift in social attitudes about the trade-off between privacy and security. This resulted in a permanently higher level of screening and surveillance. Similarly, the SARS outbreak in China in 2003 is seen as the cause of the acceleration of e-commerce, paving the way for the rise of Alibaba and other digital giants.[6]

17.4 What are the opportunities and threats?

According to our research, the disruptor pandemics creates opportunities as well as threats for organizations, which are presented in Table 17.1.

Table 17.1 The opportunities and threats

Disruptor	Pandemics
Opportunities	• Market opportunities arise in certain sectors. • Management can strengthen employee confidence through good communication and a committed approach while combatting the pandemic. • Innovation and action-orientation are enforced. • Awareness is created for sustainable employability, health, and lifelong learning, leading to sustainably deployable employees. • Employees (from affected sectors) become available for sectors where there is labor shortage.
Threats	• Employees suffer from stress, burnout, and depression as a result of higher work pressure and restrictions during the lockdown. • Management must devote much more time to combating the physical and mental consequences of the pandemic. • Affected sectors are experiencing loss of turnover, profit, and employment. • Loss of focus: a lot of process time and attention are devoted to the pandemic; planned projects, training, and improvements come to a standstill. • The short-term orientation (survival mode) temporarily takes over.

The world's largest pharmaceutical companies are still ill-prepared for future pandemics—and with it the world as a whole, which, after all, depends on those companies for drug development and vaccines. The pharmaceutical industry is working on a cure for only six of the sixteen infectious diseases with a high pandemic risk. The vast majority of drugs under development in the past years were intended to contain the COVID-19 pandemic.[7]

17.5 How do pandemics influence the megatrends?

Megatrends and disruptors do not stand alone but can, depending on the situation, strengthen or weaken each other's impact. How does a pandemic affect the other megatrends?

Technological progress can play a role in detecting pandemics and/or in measures against their further spread. An example of this is the corona app and the digital vaccination passport. Working from home and extra input or scaling down of flex workers provide relief to organizations as long as the pandemic prevails. An aging workforce poses additional risks, as older people are more vulnerable to disease, and organizations need to take more precautions for them. Migrant workers also appear to be more vulnerable to the consequences of a pandemic.

The exact influence of the corona crisis on people's skills has yet to become clear, but it is certain that the crisis will only increase the mismatch in skills. During the pandemic, many courses have been shut down, and home education is often of lower quality or less effectiveness. On the other hand, a pandemic can lead to the learning of new skills such as adaptability, stamina, and digital prowess. This will benefit organizations in the longer term, enabling them to better cope with the next pandemic. It is also clear that the pandemic has increased social inequality.

Ongoing globalization is related to pandemics in a different way. During the corona crisis, we saw that many imported goods were not available, which led to rekindling regional partnerships. There is a growing interest in local suppliers, especially of critical goods. There is also renewed attention for scarce raw materials and environmental issues. Because the economy literally came to a standstill, there were less CO_2 emissions, and some nature reserves flourished. Cities became cleaner and more livable. These unexpected positive side effects of the pandemic are seen by many as a blessing.

Chinese cosmetics company Lin Qingxuan immediately sold 9% less in its stores when many store locations were forced to close due to COVID-19, and the other stores drew far fewer passersby. In response, the company developed a strategy to digitally engage customers to replace the previous shopping experience: it gave the company's beauty consultants the role of online influencers. Thanks to this strategy, online sales soared to more than offset the drop in retail sales, especially in hard-hit Wuhan.[8]

17.6 Self-assessment

How well prepared is your organization for the future if a pandemic breaks out? With these statements from the Futurize! diagnosis (which we discuss in Chapter 18), you can determine for your organization whether it responds well to this disruptor. The statements have been developed by looking at pandemics from the perspective of the five universal HPO factors. The corresponding HPO factor is given for each statement, and we explain why it is important to aim for a good score for the statement:

- *Management quality: Management takes the right measures during a pandemic (to prevent further spread and not to endanger the employees and continuity of the company).*

  In a crisis situation, it is important that management visibly acts. Employees need guidance and a role model during these trying times. Based on the measures, employees know where they stand and what they have to do to ensure that business continuity is not jeopardized.

- *Openness and action-orientation: Employees and stakeholders are continuously informed about the effects of the pandemic.*

  Information provision gives employees clarity and peace of mind. In times of crisis, it is even more important that management is open to (one-on-one) conversations with employees to provide clarity about the situation. And as unnatural as it may sound, bad news is better than ambiguity.

- *Long-term orientation: There is a clear organizational strategy (plan of action and follow-up) to be able to continue to conduct operations during pandemics.*

  The better forethought is given about possible disruptors, such as a pandemic, the more adequately the organization can respond to new situations. Risk management is an essential part of an organization's policy.

- *Continuous improvement and renewal: The organization is looking for new ways to achieve organizational results despite the pandemic.*

  Times of crisis call for ingenuity and innovation. In some cases, this is even necessary to survive as an organization. Involve all employees in the process; every fresh look and idea is useful. Moreover, working together on solutions, using collective intelligence strategies, creates extra involvement and commitment among employees so that they are less likely to leave the organization in the future.

- *Employee quality: The organization has a continuity plan to guarantee the availability of employees during a pandemic.*

  The health and availability of employees are essential to the results of the organization. During the COVID-19 crisis, many employees dropped out for various reasons: illness, quarantine, or having to teach the children at home. This must be taken into account in the plan.

In Denmark, a corona passport has been developed to prevent the spread of corona at work. Employees who come to work must be able to show a negative test. The app collects data from the Danish health authority and checks whether the citizen has been vaccinated, has antibodies, or has recently tested negative for the coronavirus. The measure does not lead to protests among employees, even if an employer is not entitled to access to privacy-sensitive data

In Denmark, a corona passport has been developed to prevent the spread of corona at work. Employees who come to work must be able to show a negative test. The app collects data from the Danish health authority and checks whether the citizen has been vaccinated, has antibodies, or has recently tested negative for the coronavirus. The measure does not lead to protests among employees, even if an employer is not entitled to access to privacy-sensitive data.[9]

17.7 How can you prepare?

How can you ensure that your organization is constantly up-to-date and well prepared to respond to pandemics? Several courses of action emerged from our research:

- Provide a healthy work environment and take measures to minimize the risk of contamination and the spread of the pandemic. Divide employees into shifts and minimize physical contact.
- Offer employees extra support at work; think of psychological help, extra resources to get the work done, and help in their private situations. Keep in touch with employees and express your appreciation for them so that they feel seen and heard.
- Develop backup scenarios in case some employees and suppliers are unable to deliver the required performance.
- Prepare a scenario for crisis situations (these can also be caused by other disruptors), in which matters such as communication and setup of a crisis team are dealt with. By thinking about this in advance and regularly testing the crisis measures, the organization only needs to pull out the script in the event of a crisis and focus on solving the problems.

17.8 Dealing with a disruptor: the COVID-19 pandemic

In the previous chapters, we have offered quite a lot of these examples. In this section, we delve deeper into the actions that can be taken by organizations when addressing a pandemic. For this, we take the COVID-19 pandemic as our study object.[10] The COVID-19 pandemic is a typical example of a disruptor that has created a new economic and social situation. More than a year has passed since the start of the COVID-19 pandemic, and organizations have gained experience with not one but at least three epidemic waves. In order not to lose those learning experiences—especially because experts expect that COVID-19 will not be the last pandemic—we should, therefore, better prepare for new virus variants and outbreaks. So we have studied what courses of action organizations have applied in practice to combat the effects of COVID-19. We illustrate these approaches with quotes from the interviews we conducted during our research.

Research into effective COVID-19 courses of action

Our research consisted of collecting case studies of organizations that, according to themselves, dealt effectively with COVID-19. In total, we interviewed managers of 19 organizations: 13 in the Netherlands, 4 in Spain, and 2 in the UK. We had a widespread reach in terms of the industries (automotive [2], education [1], engineering [1], food [2], European government [1], healthcare [3], ICT [3], manufacturing [1], media [1], OEM [1], real estate [2], R&D [1]) and the sizes of organizations (six organizations with <100 employees, three with 101–500 employees, five with 501–1,000 employees, and five with >1,000 employees), to collect a wide variety of experiences. The interview questions we asked were as follows:

- How do you describe the impact of the COVID-19 crisis on your organization?
- What courses of action have you taken during and as a result of the COVID-19 crisis?
- What do you consider to be positive results (if any) of the COVID-19 crisis for your organization?
- What lessons have you learned from the COVID-19 crisis for the future?

The emphasis during the interviews was on collecting practices that the interviewees' organizations had applied, that is, what organizations actually did, not what they should have done, according to the interviewees. From the interviews, we collected and categorized the most effective courses of action.

At the start of the corona crisis, there was hardly any research available into how an organization could prepare for a pandemic. Since then, many studies have been started so that by now a lot of material is available. However, because the crisis was not over yet at the time of our research, we could only rely on already-proven frameworks for success when assessing the courses of action on their effectiveness. For our evaluation, we used the HPO framework because after the first COVID-19 wave, it was increasingly reported by researchers that for many organizations, the pandemic turned out to be a catalyst in the pursuit of becoming a permanently better-performing organization. The HPO framework makes it possible to evaluate the effectiveness of the COVID-19 courses of action and, with this, help organizations improve toward a sustainable higher-performing organization. The HPO framework also shows which characteristics may have been underexposed during the pandemic. In this way, we can learn from what organizations actually did in practice to deal effectively with COVID-19.[11] To this end, we selected the approaches found for their contribution to strengthening the characteristics that belong to the five factors of the HPO framework.

"We were well prepared for the coronavirus crisis, and in fact any crisis, because we put in place proven incident management procedures. We test these procedures year-round in real-world situations, such as radioactive material found at one of our sites, a crashed and leaking chemical train, or massive and sudden staff absenteeism. These incidents are portrayed through highly realistic news programs, for which we deploy real journalists, create social media feeds and use actors who play neighbors, citizens and emergency services. This testing also involves our customers and partners, so that the entire production chain can be evaluated. Through these tests, the control tools and processes are all well documented, well understood and well-practiced. This makes them familiar to all people within the organization and to our customers and partners. When COVID-19 broke out, we declared it a major incident and activated those well-practiced procedures. Within two days we had everything arranged and everything was under control."

HPO factor 1: Management quality

This concerned the extent to which the COVID-19 courses of action taken corresponded to universal characteristics of HPO managers. These managers focus on encouraging their employees' faith and trust in them; they value loyalty and live with integrity; they treat their employees with respect and maintain individual relationships with them. HPO managers are highly committed to the organization and have a strong set of ethics and standards (*relationship with employees*). They are supportive and help employees achieve results and also hold them accountable for those results (*performance focus*).

Courses of action applied during the COVID-19 pandemic

During the COVID-19 crisis, management regularly checked how employees in the organization felt and how they held out under the pressure caused by corona. They then quickly and decisively took a variety of appropriate measures to help and support employees, such as organizing activities that kept mind and body healthy. Examples included weekly "workout" sessions (in which people exchanged experiences and got rid of what was bothering them); virtual sports activities; weekly polls among employees (with questions such as "How are you?" "How are you feeling?" "How is the contact with your manager and colleagues?" and "Do you get enough information about the COVID-19 situation?"); and virtual learning sessions (on teleworking, digital development, managing virtual teams, other corona topics). In addition, many atmosphere-enhancing matters were introduced, such as fun things on the intranet (soundboard with office sounds, "show your home workplace" with selfies); regular compliments given to people who handle or work well despite COVID-19; presents/thank-you cards/personalized masks sent to the home address of employees; vlogs with employees who introduced themselves in these ("five questions to . . ."); and using humor (but not over-the-top because then one does not feel taken seriously) (*relationship with employees*).

"Our CEO started with a weekly email and video to the employees, expressing his concern for their well-being and that of their families. He gave an overview of the special measures taken by the company, such as telecommuting rules, exemptions for colleagues who are based and work from their home country, and special leave for parents. In addition, the previously quarterly news channel, on which fun and informative videos with news from and for colleagues at work are shown, is now broadcast weekly."

What was missing from this HPO factor were practices that supported the focus on performance. This was mainly reflected in decisively dealing with non-achievers. There seemed to be a general attitude that the under-performance of some employees during COVID-19 was caused by the pandemic. That is why it was often neglected to address these employees on their lagging performance and to provide them with (additional) training and/or build a file with information on the non-performance. This will create difficulties in the future when the organization accelerates and goes ahead full steam, a period in which it would need all employees to be able to fulfill promises made to customers (*performance focus*).

"There were hardly any feedback conversations with the employees who were already performing less well before the corona crisis. The fact that this leads to problems was recently shown by the fact that a major customer has entered into a partnership with one of our competitors, because he was so dissatisfied with the performance of some of our people."

HPO factor 2: Employee quality

This part of our research focused on the extent to which the COVID-19 measures taken contribute to the quality of employees. Employees in an HPO are flexible and resilient because they are well trained (formally and on-the-job) and because they are diverse as a team and, therefore, complementary. This allows them to tackle all types of problems and generate sufficient alternative ideas for improvement (*flexibility*). In addition, they are encouraged to (want to) achieve extraordinary results, which they do, among other things, by working well internally and externally (*collaboration*).

Courses of action applied during the COVID-19 pandemic

An important change in the work of employees during COVID-19 was not the content but the place where that work was performed. Many employees started working remotely from home, which made a big demand on their flexibility. After some time, organizations started looking at how they could create a good balance between working in the office and working from home (not everything has to be done at home; some things can be done safely at the office so that colleagues can have a coffee drinking moment—taking into account government health guidelines). They gave employees full flexibility to organize their own time (work versus private), and their managers showed (more) virtual and hands-off leadership (and, therefore, confidence), which was necessary because they had much less physical contact with team members (*flexibility*).

With regard to external collaboration, employees started making YouTube videos for clients and partners, showing how processes went during corona. They regularly checked with those clients and partners the effectiveness of the new processes. In addition, online collaboration platforms were set up for efficient interaction with customers/partners (*cooperation*).

> "We conduct a weekly poll among employees with questions such as: 'how do you feel?', 'how is the contact with your manager and colleagues?', 'are you receiving sufficient information about the COVID-19 situation?' Managers distribute a daily update among all employees, including the poll scores. Every morning there is a virtual stand-up in which everyone participates, with plenty of time to engage in deeper conversation. Our communication has never been so good, it really is the glue that holds the company together."

HPO factor 3: Openness and action-orientation

This part concerned the extent to which the COVID-19 courses of action taken contributed to openness and action-orientation within the organization. HPO managers value employee opinions, which they gain through frequent dialogue with employees and always involving them in important business and organizational processes; employees themselves also regularly enter into dialogue to stay in touch with each other and to exchange information (*dialogue and involvement*). Making mistakes and taking risks is always encouraged in an HPO as it is seen as valuable opportunities to learn, develop new ideas, and exchange knowledge in the pursuit of collective improvement (*willingness to change*).

Courses of action applied during the COVID-19 pandemic

During the pandemic, people emphatically came together virtually regularly to keep in touch with each other. Examples of this were as follows: a virtual lunch (literally accompanied by a sandwich, held in a pre-defined period of time, with conversations about work and private life); coffee/tea consultation (in a limited time of 20 minutes, keeping conversation to work topics and how people feel); virtual "coffee talks" of management team members with employees (to hear how things are going); a virtual "stand-up" every morning (with everyone from the department present); and virtual Friday afternoon drinks and other fun activities (virtual Easter egg hunt, virtual pub quiz, virtual bingo) (*dialogue and involvement*).

Working remotely required more frequent communication and more dialogue, especially through applications such as Skype, Microsoft Teams, and Zoom (but also the good old telephone!) so that everyone stayed in contact with each other and retained an organizational and team feeling. Ways to do this included a weekly newsletter about how the organization is doing (via email and video); frequent memos from CEO to employees (emails/vlogs) with updates on the state of affairs, developments, and measures taken; conducting "ask me anything" sessions with the management team; employees giving virtual presentations on how they dealt with corona; a "communication hub" where employees could share stories and photos; COVID-19 WhatsApp groups to monitor available capacity; continuous standby for management and HR as a source of information for employees, even outside regular working hours; and making agreements about the point of contact for employees each day (*dialogue and involvement*).

" 'Ask me anything' sessions allow people to pre-enter their questions into an application and then like their preferred questions. The more likes, the more likely the managing director and HR manager are to address the question in the hour-long session. Each session is completely packed with three hundred people and is very much appreciated, especially because there is not a presentation given as was usually done before. We definitely plan to continue with this after COVID-19."

After the first COVID-19 wave, some organizations began to rethink their purpose, setup, and role in society. This was necessary because consumers increasingly expected organizations to take more action in the aftermath of the pandemic to address environmental problems (global warming, deterioration of the natural environment, negative effects of products and services on the quality of life and the environment) and a greater focus on the continued existence of the company and the services to stakeholders in the long term (in the form of no more quarterly figures, more collaboration with clients/partners/legislators/government, more investment in environmental measures) (*willingness to change*).

A critical comment on the courses of action for this HPO factor was that in a number of organizations, the dialogue and strengthening of employee involvement turned out to depend on the proactivity of the management team, especially the CEO. This person was the one everyone was looking at and often—as in pre-COVID-19 times—now again took the lead during the pandemic. That in itself made sense, but the question was whether management team members involved employees more often than before during the pandemic. The interviewees regularly commented that they still saw too much one-way traffic: management team members standing in front of the group to address employees instead of asking questions and input and entering into a dialogue. This meant that real empowerment and better listening and the development of a learning culture, where discussing mistakes results not in scapegoating but rather in *improvements*, might not have had enough chance to develop during the pandemic.

HPO factor 4: Long-term orientation

This segment concerned the extent to which the measures taken contribute to the long-term orientation of the organization. Long-term survival is more important to an HPO than short-term profit. Stakeholders of the organization benefit from this long-term orientation and can rest assured that the organization maintains mutually beneficial long-term relationships with them (*stakeholder orientation*). An HPO is a safe and secure workplace where people feel free to contribute to the best of their ability, generally making them stay with the organization for a long time (*safety*).

Courses of action applied during the COVID-19 pandemic

During the pandemic, organizations realized that they were hugely dependent on (the goodwill of) their customers and also their cooperation partners. So they started to spend more time and effort working with their stakeholders to resolve problems caused by the pandemic. The strengthening of contact and cooperation was promoted by measures such as regular information to customers and partners about how the organization dealt with COVID-19 and how service provision was going to be guaranteed, a (minimal) office occupation that was easily accessible for clients and partners, an information portal containing a FAQ section for clients and partners, and regularly asking how customers/partners were doing and whether they needed support (*stakeholder orientation*).

"We sat down with the R&D and Innovation department to consider how we could intensify contact with customers remotely. We came up with the idea to brainstorm new products with customers via video calls. We then made samples that were sent to the customer. Subsequently we organized online tastings in which the products were inspected. I am proud to say that this has led to several new product launches, including with customers in China, Italy and England."

In addition, many health-monitoring and health-promoting measures were taken. This included an app to monitor the COVID-19 situation in the organization, additional cleaning and disinfectants in the office, posters about "1.5 meters social distancing" and "maximum number of people per room" in the office, security protocols for interacting with colleagues and clients, a virtual "HR counter" (in which the company doctor was also involved) for questions from employees, and offering free COVID-19 tests, also for family members and roommates (*safety*).

HPO factor 5: Continuous improvement and renewal

This part concerned the extent to which the COVID-19 courses of action applied contributed to the organization's continuous improvement and innovation efforts. An HPO has a unique strategy that distinguishes the organization in its sector. The organization, in this way, responds to market developments by continuously innovating its products and services and thus creating new sources of competitive advantage (*innovation*). An HPO ensures that the processes are continuously improved (faster, more efficient, more effective) and that everyone within the organization has the correct information to improve and innovate (*improvement*).

Courses of action applied during the COVID-19 pandemic

A widely shared feeling among the interviewees was that the old ways of working (e.g., being physically present in the office or factory every day) will not return (completely) when the COVID-19 pandemic is over. Organizations were, therefore, preparing themselves for an increasing number of employees continuing to work from home or remotely in virtual teams. To this end, they promoted the sharing of best practices around collaboration, flexibility, inclusion, and accountability. Measures taken to be able to work effectively remotely were as follows:

- *Technical*: accelerated introduction of video calling and meetings; making ergonomic working from home possible (providing good chairs, laptops, Wi-Fi, and other things useful for home workers); virtualizing operational processes and (going to) work with virtual teams; increasing the use of applications such as Internet of things and AI (*improvement*)
- *Process-based*: keeping (minimal) staffing at the office (based on personal preference and personal circumstances of people and using a rotation schedule) that was easily accessible for colleagues working from home; a (virtual) service desk to support working from home; holding "office garden" sessions (where employees simultaneously logged in to do their work together); installing an information portal containing a FAQ section for employees (*improvement*)

In addition, operational processes were critically reviewed in order to introduce more speed and efficiency in them. The latter was achieved by looking at the quality of the end-to-end delivery processes ("the client journey") to make them more resilient, agile, and automated; redesigning supply chains (especially for critical materials) to better ensure availability; delegating more and empowering lower organizational levels to speed up decision-making and implementation; flattening of the organizational structure (and thus simplification) with more flexible teams and hybrid ways of working; creating "slack" in business operations so that there was extra capacity to deal with unexpected events (*innovation*).

> "Whereas the normal course of business before the crisis was 'we've always done it this way,' new solutions are now being sought. Consultations are taking place differently, contact with clients is much more digital and colleagues now work more from home. These changes were sometimes realized within days. It didn't always go right the first time, but we called this 'failing forward': we learn from mistakes to do better next time. Everyone contributed from their own knowledge and everyone was heard; the hierarchical 'layers' became less important."

A critical remark regarding the courses of action for this HPO factor was that, in general, it is very important that organizations continue to innovate and not just put out fires caused by the changed situation. On the contrary, they must make strategic use of the new situation, as an opportunity and burning platform, for innovation. So not only react reactively but react proactively. However, during the pandemic, quite a few organizations stopped innovative projects because of the assumption that there was no time left for those projects because all attention had to go to crisis management. The rebuilding of the company at a number of organizations also started after the first COVID-19 wave (summer 2020), but this came to a standstill at the time of the second wave (after the summer). It is expected that this will (hopefully) be picked up again when the pandemic is (almost) over (*renewal, improvement*).

Difference between the first (before summer 2020) and second (after summer 2020) COVID-19 wave

At the time of writing this book, we had experienced the second and third COVID-19 waves. A brief check that we conducted at a number of the organizations previously surveyed showed that many of the aforementioned learning experiences had been fully useful during the third wave. The organizations not only continued their measures but also took the learning experiences of other organizations to heart. The check did reveal a number of differences between the first and second waves. During the first wave, the managers interviewed experienced a sense of unreality as they looked for ways to make their teams work virtually and wondered how they could stay in touch with their people as they started working remotely. At the same time, they had a sense of calm "because we can't do much right now"—many meetings with customers and partners were canceled. During the first wave, organizations hardly knew what was going on, and there was no sense of time: they didn't know how long it would take. Some organizations were right on top of it and switched quickly; others took so long that they were constantly running behind the facts. In the first case, productivity increased, contrary to expectations, because people spent less time commuting, and virtual meetings turned out to be quite effective.

"In the first wave, everything was unreal, you were looking for how Teams worked, how to connect with other people. Now, in the second wave, we know how Teams works and the whole agenda is, as usual, completely filled with appointments. You press 'Leave' and immediately go into the next meeting, so you just keep working. You used to have a break in between, get a coffee or go to the toilet, now you go on and on. In the first wave you often heard: 'I'm having a break,' now you mainly hear: 'I'm so busy.' There are so many possibilities to do something, you go from virtual meeting to virtual meeting. It's almost business-as-usual, I really have to schedule my breaks."

In the second wave, the experiences were different. Organizations had learned during the first wave not to wait but to act faster. We saw many more to-go restaurants and more products offered online. Employees were kept working elsewhere where possible (restaurant staff went to work in maintenance for a bicycle manufacturer, for example), and regional initiatives were launched, such as test streets and "support your local businesses." Because everyone was now used to working virtually, everyone's agenda was filled as in the pre-COVID-19 days. The regular busyness was partly caused by almost everyone showing up for appointments, virtual but increasingly also physical. This period largely coincided with the closing of schools and the heavy burden on parents to educate their children at home. Many people had enough of this by that time; they wanted (more) physical contact with other people again. It was striking that in some cases, the productivity gains previously achieved were lost again. Reasons for this were the fatigue in people who had not fully recovered between the first and second waves and the fact that some productivity gains were optical because they were caused by people not actually working more efficiently but longer (they now filled in travel time with extra work).

Finally

What is the common thread that becomes visible when we look at all the described actions? We believe that during a crisis, it is especially important to continue to listen to and support employees. Take the greatest care of the physical and mental health of employees so that they remain employable. As a manager, make sure that you are constantly reachable and available. Hear what the employees have to say, both in face-to-face conversations and in virtual sessions. Follow up on what employees tell you and involve them in developing solutions. Even in difficult times, set challenging goals but make sure that the employees do not become stressed; after all, one person can handle more than the other. Show your human side; no one is infallible. We dare to say that implementation of the above leads to excellent performance, also during a pandemic.

Because of the experiences gained during, we now know better how to act in the event of the next pandemic. But let's not make the mistake of thinking that we are "in the clear" with the lessons learned. In fact, it is now time to think ahead. As a result of the pandemic, we can expect new challenges. Have you already thought about what these are? For example, how do you deal with the increasing number of employees/

customers/suppliers who are getting into financial problems? Or how do you deal with employees/customers/suppliers who suffer from (long-term) health problems as a result of COVID-19 ("long COVID-19")? In any case, organizations should better prepare for other disruptors (such as environmental problems and disasters or IT hacks) by establishing a dynamic Futurizing process—that is, a process by which an organization prepares for the future—which fosters forward-thinking. Everyone's job is to think ahead and be proactive, rather than reactive, as was the prevalent case with COVID-19.

> "The start of the pandemic coincided with the introduction of a new future-proof job classification system for our organization. Initially, opinions were divided about what a future-oriented job classification entailed. For example, we had included the following responsibilities for all employees in our role profiles: 'Keep up with professional knowledge, trends and developments. Regularly take some distance from daily work and translate what you have learned into improvement or innovation of products, services or processes.' In other words, it's everyone's turn, not just management, when it comes to preparing for the next crisis. This shared responsibility is now understood by everyone!"

Notes

1 Boutellier (2021)
2 Kavanagh et al. (2019/2020)
3 Larson en Nigmatulina (2010)
4 Calero and Soledad (2020)
5 Karabag (2020)
6 Jacobides and Reeves (2020)
7 Berkhout and Hensen (2021)
8 Jacobides and Reeves (2020)
9 Hueck (2021)
10 This section is based on Waal et al. (2021).
11 Hishan (2020)

Chapter 18

The Futurize! process

Now that the most influential megatrends and disruptor and their (potential) impacts on organizations are known, it is time for you to look at the process with which your organization can future-ready itself. This is done in three steps that together form a cycle (see Figure 18.1):

1   Conduct the Futurize! diagnosis.
2   Formulate the Futurize! action plan.
3   Execute the Futurize! action plan and monitor the results.

Developing the Futurize! diagnosis

In order to arrive at a practical process with which an organization can make itself future-ready, we organized two roundtable discussions with experienced managers. The reason to use a group of experts is that they bring knowledge, authority, and insight to a topic and that a group of experts can produce more wisdom than just one expert. Such a group of experts is often brought together in roundtable discussions where they exchange opinions, knowledge, views, and ideas in a time-efficient and effective manner. The experts originated from our networks and were selected on the length of work experience and an organizational role that provided them with a viewpoint on strategic developments of their organization. The reason to conduct *two* roundtables was that this afforded the opportunity for participants of the second roundtable to build on the results of the first roundtable, thus raising the overall quality of the roundtable results. The first roundtable yielded a first draft of the process to make the organization future-ready, a process that was dubbed Futurize! During the second roundtable, this process was refined and optimized. We then conducted pilots with the draft

DOI: 10.4324/9781003273264-18

Futurize! process at five organizations: a healthcare provider, an accountancy firm, a multinational food company, a governmental agency, and a raw material producer. Each pilot built on the results of the previous pilot so that the diagnosis and especially the future-readiness process were refined until we could arrive at the process depicted in Figure 18.1.

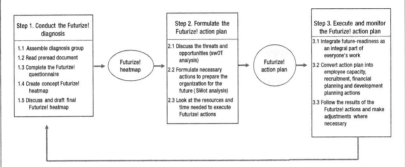

Figure 18.1 Schematic representation of the Futurize! diagnose process

The term *Futurizing* accurately conveys its meaning: it is taking the organization into the future.[1] It is not an activity that happens once a year or quarterly, but it is a continuous and active way of thinking about what is to come, with agility and flexibility, which is more a behavior than a system.[2]

18.1 Step 1: Conduct the Futurize! diagnosis

Step 1 starts with selecting the people in the organization who have a good idea of what is going on internally and of the work processes. These selected people are often management team members supplemented with specialists and, for instance, representatives of the work council. It is advisable to include views and insights from managers/experts and targeted users throughout the process. To ensure that all insights are gathered and, in a later stage, broadly accepted, it is advisable to invite stakeholders from all organizational levels and areas of expertise and with different ways of thinking ("embrace the maverick"). Dissenting opinions should be welcomed and encountered in an open manner. Do not filter opinions too early! Having each participant fill in the question-naire first ensures that valuable opinions do not get lost or become biased due to groupthink.

Each of the participants of the diagnosis gets a pre-read document in which they find the following information needed before they start filling in the Futurize! questionnaire: a description of the megatrends and the disruptor to be scored, a definition of the concepts used, and a description of the various activities conducted during the Futurize! diagnosis. The participants then fill in the Internet-based Futurize! questionnaire. In this questionnaire, the participants are asked to score each megatrend and disruptor on the following:

- *Estimated degree of impact:* According to the participant's estimate, how big will the impact of the megatrend or disruptor be on the functioning and results of the organization? This impact can be negative but possibly also positive.
- *Level of preparation:* How well does the organization proactively prepare for the impact of a megatrend/disruptor, according to the participant? This includes the activities we described for each megatrend and disruptor in the "Self-assessment" section of each chapter.
- *Estimated degree of preparation:* According to the participant's estimate, how well prepared is the organization for the occurrence of a megatrend or disruptor? In other words, it is an estimate of the effectiveness of the actions that the organization has taken to deal with the impact of the megatrend/disruptor.

The participants not only do this for the thirteen megatrends and one disruptor but also for sector trends. They can, during the diagnosis, add these sector trends as they see them developing in the sector their organization operates in. Based on the summarized score of the participants, a draft Futurize! heat map is constructed. A heat map is a two-dimensional chart with, on the y-axis, the estimated degree of impact of each megatrend/disruptor and, on the x-axis, the estimated degree of preparedness for each megatrend/disruptor (see Figure 18.2).

Based on the average scores for estimated degree impact and preparedness respectively,[3] each megatrend /disruptor ends up in one of six areas in the draft Futurize! heat map. Each area differs in the sense of urgency with which the organization has to prepare itself on a particular megatrend or disruptor. When a megatrend/disruptor has, according to the participants, a low impact on the organization while its preparedness for this megatrend/disruptor is also low ("Monitor area" in the left-hand bottom corner in Figure 18.2), the organization in principle only has to monitor the megatrend/disruptor in case it becomes more urgent regarding its impact; until then, no further action is needed. On the other end of the spectrum, the organization also has to monitor a megatrend/disruptor, which has a high impact and for which it is well-prepared ("Monitor area" in the top right-hand corner). In this case, the monitoring is for

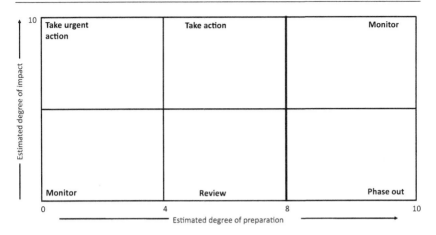

Figure 18.2 The Futurize! heat map

how well the actions the organization is taking to address the particular megatrend/disruptor are working out.

When a megatrend/disruptor has a low impact but the organization is very well prepared, it can be inferred this might be overpreparedness, and the organization can tone down or even abandon some of its efforts for this particular megatrend/disruptor ("Phase out area" in bottom right-hand corner). Again, on the other end, when a megatrend/disruptor has a high impact but the organization is not well prepared for this megatrend/disruptor, the organization should take immediate and urgent action to prepare itself in the shortest term possible ("Take urgent action area" in the top left-hand corner). When the organization is "average" prepared (between 4 and 8 on the x-axis) for a megatrend/disruptor while this megatrend/disruptor has a low impact, the organization can consider reducing its efforts for this megatrend/disruptor and start monitoring it ("Review area" in the bottom middle). In contrast, when this megatrend/disruptor has a high impact, the organization has to take action to address it ("Take action" area in the top middle).

The draft heat map forms the input for a discussion in a larger group of representatives of the organization. During the discussion, each megatrend and disruptor is evaluated on its impact—which can be either positive or negative (opportunity and threat, respectively, in a SWOT analysis)—and degree of preparedness. This discussion can lead the participants to change the position of the megatrend/disruptor in the heat map. The finalized Futurize! heat map depicts the priority with which the megatrends and the disruptor need to be tackled by the organization.

Tips

- Ensure that senior management emphasizes the importance of the Futurize! process and actively participates in the process.
- Invest time in getting to know each other. This may be perceived as a slow start to the process, but you will benefit from a better understanding of everyone's point of view.
- Share the results and actions of the Futurize! diagnosis with the organization so that everyone knows and understands what its status is with regard to its future-readiness.
- Incorporate the Futurize! process into the annual strategy and budget cycle, not as an add-on process but as an integrated aspect that is dealt with in a multidisciplinary manner.
- Get representatives from different parts of the organization to participate. In this way, as many trends as possible are picked up, which can then be discussed and prioritized.
- Stories and experiences may be just as important as numbers and facts. Stay open-minded.
- Include employees in the Futurize! process so that broad attention for and knowledge about thinking about the future is created within the organization. In this way, the collective cleverness (knowledge and ideas) of the entire organization is used, and ownership for the results of the Futurize! process is created throughout the organization.

18.2 Step 2: Formulate the Futurize! action plan

As soon as there is a mutually agreed picture of the current situation, step 2 follows: formulating an action plan. The Futurize! action plan provides an overview of the actions that need to be taken to prepare the organization for the future, to defend itself against threats or to seize opportunities. When drawing up the action plan, the current status of the organization is taken into account, with regard to resources, budget, and time available to carry out the actions—strengths and weaknesses in a SWOT analysis—so that the resulting action plan is realistic.

Tips

- Formulate a vision for the future and a purpose for the organization together with stakeholders. This provides direction for the long term.
- Organize a process with employees to jointly determine the agenda and action plan for the future. Ensure that policy and execution are not detached (e.g., separate processes) and are tested in an early phase. But not too early, before any result can be expected.

- Be transparent about the choices made; communicate these within the organization.
- Free up budget and time to be able to realize the formulated actions. If an initiative does not deliver the expected output, do not scapegoat or blame anyone. Just move on and try to find a solution that does work.
- Teach employees to be future-oriented (to Futurize!) so that this becomes a habit to them.

18.3 Step 3: Execute and monitor the Futurize! action plan

Finally, in step 3, the action map is executed. This is done by integrating the Futurize! actions in the daily practice of the organization, at a realistic pace based on the capacity, recruitment, financial planning, and development planning of employees. During the execution of the action plan, the plan is regularly updated based on current circumstances and events and the progress of the actions.

Tips

- As management, create a safe and entrepreneurial working environment with clear core values such as integrity and respect.
- Keep a close eye on the results of the Futurize! actions. For example, develop a dashboard that allows you to monitor progress. Safeguard that knowledge is shared broadly within the ecosystem. Regularly ask yourself whether the results achieved contribute sufficiently to the future-readiness of the organization.
- Investigate the possibilities of taking actions together with suppliers, customers, and fellow companies (in the sector) aimed at making the value chain and sector future-ready.
- Provide space to the organization to develop new ideas. Support suggestions for improvement and experiments aimed at the future. Allow mistakes but also hold employees to their responsibilities when executing the Futurize! actions in a timely and proper manner.
- Be flexible and expect changes in action plans. Make use of decision-making practices and tools (strategic foresight) to recognize the situation you are facing as an organization. Look for cooperation instead of trying to solve everything on your own.
- In conversations with employees, include as a standard question what they need to remain successful in the future, and support them in carrying out the Futurize! actions.

There are significant differences in annual reports, according to research by accountant KPMG. One Amsterdam Exchange Index (AEX) company mentioned eight risks in their annual report, another report mentioned 44 risks. And 18 AEX companies had not identified a pandemic and the subsequent economic shock as a risk. Another point of criticism: companies do not rank the risks (which are the real and relevant threats), the study shows. Companies are especially aware of short-term risks; events that liwe further in time and calamities (e.g., explosion, flooding) are rarely discussed.[4]

The Futurize! diagnosis at Food Preparation Ltd.

Food Preparation Ltd.[5] is a supplier to the food industry with ingredients needed to produce specific food products. As part of a bigger conglomerate, the company operates worldwide but focuses mainly on Europe and the Americas. Despite receiving strategic guidelines from the mother company, the organization can by and large set its own strategic course. The company decided to participate in the Futurize! diagnosis as part of its journey toward becoming an HPO and its continuing efforts to raise the quality of its risk management process. Members of the management team filled in the Futurize! questionnaire and partook in the subsequent discussion. Food Preparation Ltd.'s Futurize! heat map is shown in Figure 18.3.

Food Preparation Ltd.'s heat map shows the position of the thirteen megatrends and the disruptor, supplemented with three sector-specific megatrends (new production techniques, legal changes, personalized food). The heat map indicates that the discussion participants acknowledged one urgent-to-be-addressed megatrend: workforce composition. They were of the opinion that the increasingly shorter employment contracts posed a risk to the continuity of the organization. One of the participants had worked all her life, in various positions, at Food Preparation Ltd. As a result, knowledge had been retained in the organization over a long period of

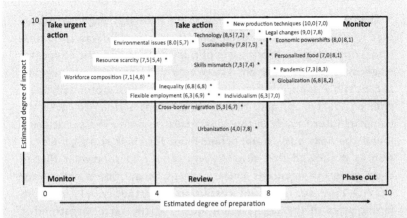

Figure 18.3 The Futurize! heatmap of the Food Preparation Ltd. case study

time. However, she was an exception as shorter employment contracts seemed to become the norm for the new generations. The participants agreed that not only should they take a better look at ways to keep employees tied to the organization, but they should also find better methods to safeguard knowledge and processes.

Most megatrends were in the "Take action" area of the heat map. This was caused by the realization among the participants that despite the organization being quite busy with addressing these megatrends, this was far from enough. As one participant put it, "Being busy with a lot of things does not mean you actually achieve success in at least one thing." As an example, the megatrend "skills mismatch" was given where the company undertook a lot of things, such as setting up in-house training programs for employees and traineeships. However, the discussion during the diagnosis revealed that many participants were of the opinion that real craftsmanship was increasingly missing, especially in the production and R&D departments and that more effort was needed there. Fortunately, the organization had reacted quite adequately to the disruptor "pandemic," as shown by the participants putting it in the top right-hand "Monitor" area. Two megatrends warranted a closer review ("Cross-border migration" and "Urbanization") as the participants were not sure about the direction these megatrends would take for their organization. Thus, further investigation was needed.

The participants, in their review of the Futurize! diagnosis, stated that it would be useful, seeing that their company was a multinational operating in various parts of the world, to conduct a separate diagnosis per world region. This would take into account regional and possibly even local circumstances and, thus, potentially yield different heat maps and, therefore, different actions to make the company future-ready in those particular regions. The participants found the heat map an important input for their strategic discussion as it showed that several megatrends had somewhat slipped their attention in recent times, perhaps because of the disruptor COVID-19. Also, it was interesting to them that people from different parts of the organization looked at the same megatrend in different ways; thus, the diagnosis formed a good "breeding ground" for exchanging information and viewpoints and coming closer together as a team.

The Futurize! diagnosis at Healthcare Organization

Healthcare Organization (HCO) is a nationally operating organization that provides multiple forms of healthcare. For example, clients are received in clinics or at walk-in locations, while a lot of ambulatory care (home care) is also provided. The organization is divided into regions, each of which has a large number of teams. Each team is led by a team manager and a medical specialist, who together manage a group of healthcare providers. HCO had been developing into an HPO for some time, but like all healthcare organizations, its work was severely affected by the corona pandemic. From one day to the next, HCO had to transform itself into an organization that mainly provided care from a distance, with team members mainly working from home. In a traditionally conservative industry, this was quite the switch. HCO wanted to conduct the Futurize! diagnosis to determine where the organization was at that moment and how it could better prepare for the future so that a similar event like corona would have less impact. A number of management team members, staff, regional managers, and team managers completed

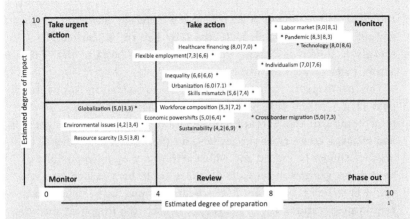

Figure 18.4 The Futurize! heatmap of the HCO case study

the Futurize! questionnaire and took part in the ensuing discussion. The Futurize! heat map of HCO is given in Figure 18.4.

HCO's heat map shows the position of the thirteen megatrends and the disruptor, supplemented by two sector-specific megatrends (changing healthcare financing and a difficult labor market [i.e., growing staff shortages]). While reviewing the heat map, a discussion immediately arose among the participants. They asked each other what they understood by the speed of technological developments and, in that light, its placing in the area at the top right of the heat map ("Monitor"). A number of participants stated that it was true that steps had been taken in the area of dealing with technological developments, but they doubted whether the organization as a whole was already "in the green" in this respect. As an example, it was cited that many employees still had difficulty with a simple Teams meeting. Another example was the attitude in some places within the organization regarding remote care or providing care advice through virtual means: the moment the (first) lockdown was over, many colleagues went back to the old method of a physical consultation. Of course, remote or virtual care is not always possible, but the lockdown period would have been an opportunity to make this a regular part of care provision. After discussion, participants agreed that "well prepared" was really only a qualification of the opportunity in this area, but it did not necessarily mean that the mindset of employees to leverage technological innovations was already there. It was noted that it was not just about mindset, but this kind of technology also required a different leadership style and different management skills that still had to be learned. They, therefore, shifted this trend from the "Monitor" area to the "Take action" area in the heat map.

The participants concluded that the conversation about the heat map was actually more important than the heat map itself. In a method of the Socratic conversation, one can gain insight—and perhaps come closer together—on the question of where the urgencies must be placed and which actions are really important to help the organization further. A status could be awarded to each trend (1 = being considered, 2 = being planned, 3 = implementation in preparation, 4 = in progress). In fact, the first heat map is a kind of pre-advice, and through the discussion, one comes to a more accurate heat map. It was noted that it is very valuable to go through such a process. The participants also suggested that within HCO, in addition to input from management and staff departments, input could also be requested from the client council and the works council in order to collect as much information as possible. Requesting this broad input in advance takes more time, but there is a greater chance that the actions arising from the heat map will be better understood and, therefore, have broader support in the organization. One suggestion was to process the outcome of the Futurize! process in a document or other form of communication towards the organization—following the example of the strategic brief that is widely used within healthcare organizations.

The Futurize! diagnosis at Drinky Ltd.

Drinky Ltd. is an organization with approximately 100 employees (global sales, research and development, operations, staff) that develops and produces drinks for the B2B ingredients market. The company has a global growth strategy. Drinky got through the corona period quite well. All measures were taken to keep distance so that the staff could continue to work in a safe environment. The production and delivery of products remained stable and even increased slightly. The company found itself, therefore, in a good and healthy financial position. Drinky's managers had signed up for the Futurize! workshop because they thought it would be interesting to go through such a process with a number of people. In the past, various participants were accustomed to periodically

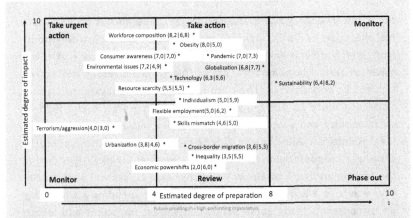

Figure 18.5 The Futurize! heatmap of the Drinky Ltd. case study

carrying out an evaluation of the organization with the risk management department and the various business units. As a result, not much explanation was needed about what the Futurize! diagnosis would entail. The Futurize! questionnaire was sent to all MT members, as well as to the heads of functional areas, such as purchasing and quality. In addition, a representative of the works council was asked to participate. The participants found it interesting to fill in the questionnaire; there were no comments that this was difficult or that the questions were illegible. Completing the questionnaire actually made the participants curious about what the results would be and also got them thinking about the future-readiness of Drinky.

During the workshop, the Futurize! heat map was first reviewed (see Figure 18.5). For seven megatrends and the disruptor, the participants estimated that these would have (or already had) a significant impact on Drinky and that the organization was not yet sufficiently prepared for this ("Take action" area in the heat map). In addition, the participants mentioned a number of additional sector trends—namely, attention to health/obesity, consumer awareness about food in general, and possible terrorism or aggression in the food sector. During the evaluation of the diagnosis, the participants noted that the approach with a self-assessment, heat map, and action plan was a good fit with activities that must be carried out for the food industry's FSCC/ISO 22000 standard. In addition to certification, every food company is obliged to periodically carry out a risk inventory and evaluation (RI&E). The output of the Futurize! diagnosis could be included in this RI&E scan. A learning point from the pilot was that it is useful to make an inventory of these types of trajectories in advance; in this way, processes and activities can be coordinated. The output of the Futurize! diagnosis could also contribute to achieving certification programs in the field of sustainability and sustainable employability initiatives; think of the UTC Rainforest Alliance and Cocoa Horizons. The Futurize! workshop was scheduled during a very busy week at Drinky, right during the implementation of a new company-wide IT system application. This was also a learning point: the thought of spending a whole day on a workshop made some participants a bit impatient and led to some last-minute cancellations. The Futurize! diagnosis is probably best as part of or in preparation for the annual strategy days.

18.4 Final words

Organizations can better prepare for the megatrends and the disruptor with the information from this book and by means of a dynamic Futurize! process. It is now a question of developing and implementing a process whereby the organization prepares for the future, and thinking ahead as a skill is emphatically stimulated in its people. In our opinion, to futurize should be the new verb for managers.

Everyone's job is to think ahead and be proactive (rather than reactive, as was the case with COVID-19). An example of this is one of the organizations we interviewed, which has now included the following responsibilities for all employees in its role profiles: "Stay abreast with professional knowledge, trends, and developments. Regularly distance yourself from daily work for a while and translate what you have learned into improvement or innovation of products, services, or processes." In other words, everyone—and not just management—is responsible for preparing for the next crisis.

Good luck with Futurizing!

Notes

1 Morgan (2020)
2 Smith (2020)
3 Although averages are presented in the heat map, it can be insightful to present the separate, deviating scores as well.
4 Leijten and Tamminga (2021)
5 Upon request, we anonymized the pilot organizations and also modified their Futurize! heat maps to protect confidentiality.

References

Anani, N. (2018), 'Paving the way for the future of work'. In: *Canadian Public Policy*, Vol. 44 Issue S1, pp. S167–S176.

Annunziata, M. & H. Bourgeois (2018), 'The future of work: How G20 countries can leverage digital-industrial innovations into stronger high-quality jobs growth'. In: *Economics: The Open-Access, Open-Assessment E-Journal*, Vol. 12 Issue 42, pp. 1–23.

Anthes, E. (2017), 'The shape of work to come'. In: *Nature News*, Vol. 550 Issue 7676, p. 316.

Appel-Meulenbroek, H.A.J.A., S.M.C. Vosters, A.D.A.M. Kemperman & T.A. Arentze (2019), *Workplace needs and their support; are millennials different from other generations?*. Paper presented at the twenty fifth annual Pacific Rim Real Estate Society conference (PRRES 2019), Melbourne, Australia.

Bakhshi, H., J.M. Downing, M.A. Osborne & P. Schneider (2017), *The future of skills: Employment in 2030*. Pearson, London.

Balliester, T., & A. Elsheikhi (2018), The future of work: a literature review. *ILO Research Department Working Paper*, 29, 1–62.

Batt, R. (2018), 'The financial model of the firm, the "future of work", and employment relations'. In: A. Wilkinson, T. Dundon, J. Donaghey & A. Colvin (eds.), *The Routledge companion to employment relations*. Routledge, London, pp. 465–479.

Beech, N. & F. Anseel (2020), 'COVID-19 and its impact on management research and education: Threats, opportunities and a manifesto'. In: *British Journal of Management*, Vol. 31 Issue 3, pp. 447–449.

Behrendt, C. & Q.A. Nguyen (2019), 'Ensuring universal social protection for the future of work'. In: *Transfer: European Review of Labour and Research*, Vol. 25 Issue 2, pp. 205–219.

Bell, M., D. Bristow & S. Martin (2017), *The future of work in Wales*. Wales Centre for Public Policy: www.wcpp.org.uk/publication/future-of-work-in-wales/.

Benjamin, J. (2021), 'De gekte voorbij, ook na de crisis [Beyond the madness, even after the crisis]'. In: *NRC*, 5 January, pp. 10–11.

Berkhout, K. & C. Hensen (2021), 'Farmaciebedrijven zijn niet ingesteld op nieuwe pandemie [Pharmaceutical companies are not prepared for new pandemics]'. In: *NRC*, 27 January, pp. 12–13.

Bhalla, V., S. Dyrchs & R. Strack (2017), *Twelve forces that will radically change how organizations work*. BCG Perspectives, The Boston Consulting Group, Boston.

Bhargava, R. (2020), *Non obvious megatrends: How to see what others miss and predict the future*. Ideapress Publishing: www.ideapresspublishing.com.

Biswas, A.K., C. Tortajada & P. Rohner (eds.) (2018), *Assessing global water megatrends*. Springer, Singapore.

Bokkum, M. van & M. Kuiper (2021), 'Een oude medicijnfabriek stof je niet zomaar af [You don't just dust off an old medicine factory]'. In: *NRC*, 27–28 February, pp. E14–E15.

Boutellier, H. (2021), 'Het virus blijft: Bespreek de langetermijnstrategie [The virus remains: Discuss the long-term strategy]'. In: *NRC*, 2 February, p. 19.

Bowers, M.R., J.R. Hall & M.M. Srinivasan (2017), 'Organizational culture and leadership style: The missing combination for selecting the right leader for effective crisis management'. In: *Business Horizons*, Vol. 60 Issue 4, pp. 551–563.

Bradbury, R.B., S.H.M. Butchart, B. Fisher, F.M.R. Hughes, L. Ingwall-King, M.A. MacDonald, J.C. Merriman, K.S.H. Peh, A.S. Pellier, D.H.L. Thomas, R. Trevelyan & A. Balmford (2021), 'The economic consequences of conserving or restoring sites for nature'. In: *Nature Sustainability*: https://doi.org/10.1038/s41893-021-00692-9.

Brougham, D. & J. Haar (2018), 'Smart technology, artificial intelligence, robotics, and algorithms (STARA): Employees' perceptions of our future workplace'. In: *Journal of Management & Organization*, Vol. 24 Issue 2, pp. 239–257.

Brugh, M. aan den (2021), 'Zo gaat de wereld de opwarming nooit verslaan [The world will never beat global warming this way]'. In: *NRC*, 25 January, pp. 6–9.

Burkle, F.M. (2010), 'Do pandemic preparedness planning systems ignore critical community and local-level operational challenges?'. In: *Disaster Medicine and Public Health Preparedness*, Vol. 4 Issue 1, pp. 24–29.

Calero, D. & M. Soledad (2020), 'An x-ray of pandeconomics: A look at pandemics past puts corona crisis in perspective'. In: *Caribbean Business*, Vol. 6 Issue 10, pp. 8–11.

Cambridge Dictionary (2020): https://dictionary.cambridge.org/dictionary/english/disruptor?q=disruptors.

Campbell, Stacy M., Jean M. Twenge & W. Keith Campbell (2017), 'Fuzzy but useful constructs: Making sense of the differences between generations, work, aging and retirement'. In: *Work, Aging and Retirement*, Vol. 3 Issue 2, pp. 130–139.

Cassells, R., A. Duncan, A. Mavisakalyan, J. Phillimore, R. Seymour & Y. Tarverdi (2018), *Future of work in Australia: Preparing for tomorrow's world*. BCEC Report, Bankwest Curtin Economics Centre, Perth.

CBI (2020), *Combatting workplace inequality: The intersectional approach*: www.cbi.org.uk/articles/combatting-workplace-inequality-the-intersectional-approach/.

CBS (2017), *Worden we individualistischer? [Are we becoming more individualistic?]*: www.cbs.nl/nl-nl/nieuws/2017/52/worden-we-individualistischer-.

Cheung-Judge, M. (2017), 'Future of organizations and implications for OD practitioners, summary'. In: *OD Practitioner*, Vol. 49 Issue 3, pp. 7–13.

Choi, J., M. Dutz & Z. Usman (2019), *The future of work in africa harnessing the potential of digital technologies for all: A companion to the world development report 2019 on the changing nature of work*. World Bank Group, Washington, DC.

Choudhury, P. (2020), 'Our work-from-anywhere future'. In: *Harvard Business Review*, Vol. 98 Issue 6, pp. 58–67.

Cobouw (2020), 'Japanse bouwer neemt Jan Snel over: "Dit is een serieus dingetje"' [Japanese builder takes over Jan Snel: "This is a serious thing"]'. *Cobouw*: www.cobouw.nl/marktontwikkeling/nieuws/2020/12/japanse-bouwer-neemt-jan-snel-over-dit-is-een-serieus-dingetje-101291551.

Colombino, U. (2019), 'Is unconditional basic income a viable alternative to other social welfare measures?'. *IZA World of Labor*, Vol. 2.

CompanyMatch (2016), *Individualisering moet ook doorklinken in werk-en privébalans [Individualization must also be reflected in work and private balance]*: www.companymatch.me/news/nederlands/individualisering-moet-ook-doorklinken-werk-en-privebalans/.

Cook, J.W. (ed.) (2019), *Sustainability, human well-being, and the future of education*. Palgrave Macmillan, London.

Cook, N. (2017), *Enterprise 2.0. How social software will change the future of work*. Routledge, London.

Diamandis, P.H. & S. Kotler (2020), *The future is faster than you think: How converging technologies are transforming business, industries, and our lives*. Simon & Schuster Paperbacks, New York.

Dignan, A. (2019), *Brave new work: Are you ready to reinvent your organization?*. Penguin, London.

Dijk, B. van (2020), 'Bedrijven vergroenen steeds meer via een virtuele stroomdeal [Companies are increasingly greening through a virtual power deal]'. In: *Het Financieele Dagblad*, 22 December.

Dijk, B. van (2021), 'Energiecrisis Texas door extreem weer en slechte planning [Texas energy crisis due to extreme weather and poor planning]'. In: *Het Financieele Dagblad*, 17 February.

Diong, T. (2017), 'The future of management systems'. In: *Quality Magazine*, September, pp. 52–54.

Do, T. & N. Mai (2020), 'High-performance organization: A literature review'. In: *Journal of Strategy and Management*, Vol. 13 Issue 2, pp. 297–309.

Doorn, N. van (2017), 'Platform labor: On the gendered and racialized exploitation of low-income service work in the "on-demand' economy"'. In: *Information, Communication & Society*, Vol. 20 Issue 6, pp. 898–914.

Eggers, F. (2020), 'Masters of disasters? Challenges and opportunities for SMEs in times of crisis'. In: *Journal of Business Research*, Vol. 116, pp. 199–208.

Erboz, G. (2017), *How to define industry 4.0: Main pillars of industry 4.0*. Paper presented during the 7th International Conference on Management (ICoM 2017), Nita, Slovakia.

Esposito, M. & T. Tse (2018), 'DRIVE: The five megatrends that underpin the future business, social, and economic landscapes'. In: *Thunderbird International Business Review*, Vol. 60 Issue 1, pp. 121–129.

FD (2021a), 'Unilever wil leefbaar loon bij leveranciers [Unilever wants a living wage from suppliers]'. In: *Het Financieele Dagblad*, 22 January, p. 14.

FD (2021b), 'BNP Paribas ageert tegen ontbossing [BNP Paribas takes action against deforestation]'. In: *Het Financieele Dagblad*, 16 February.

Florito, J., U. Aneja & M.B. de Sanfeliu (2018), *A future of work that works for women.* G20 Insights, Berlin.

Fuller, J., M. Raman, A. Bailey & N. Vaduganathan (2020), 'Rethinking the on-demand workforce'. In: *Harvard Business Review*, Vol. 98 Issue 6, pp. 96–103.

Fuller, J.B., M. Raman, J.K. Wallenstein & A. de Chalendar (2019), 'Your workforce is more adaptable than you think'. In: *Harvard Business Review*, Vol. 97 Issue 3, pp. 118–126.

Gallup en Bates College (2019), *Forging pathways to purposeful work: The role of higher education.* Gallup, Washington DC.

Global Deal (2020), *The global deal for decent work and inclusive growth flagship report 2020: Social dialogue, skills and COVID-19.* The Global Deal for Decent Work and Inclusive Growth: www.theglobaldeal.com.

Godwin, C. (2019), 'The £7,500 dress that does not exist'. *BBC News*: www.bbc.com/news/business-49794403.

Gratton, L. (2020a), 'The pandemic's lessons for managing uncertainty'. In: *MIT Sloan Management Review*: https://sloanreview.mit.edu/article/the-pandemics-lessons-for-managing-uncertainty/.

Gratton, L. (2020b), 'Five insights from Davos on the future of work'. In: *MIT Sloan Management Review*: https://sloanreview.mit.edu/article/five-insights-from-davos-on-the-future-of-work/.

Gruen, D. (2017), 'The future of work'. In: *Policy: A Journal of Public Policy and Ideas*, Vol. 33 Issue 3, pp. 3–8.

Guttal, S. (2010), 'Globalisation'. In: *Development in Practice*, Vol. 17 Issue 4–5, pp. 1–10.

Hajkowicz, S.A., H. Cook & A. Littleboy (2012), *Our future world: Global megatrends that will change the way we live, the 2012 revision.* Commonwealth Scientific and Industrial Research Organization CSIRO, Australia.

Harteis, C. (2018), *The impact of digitalization in the workplace.* Springer, Cham.

Hartog-de Wilde, S. den (2019), *Bioprinters, grondstof-rotondes en brainternet? Hoe wij produceren, consumeren en herverdelen in 2050* [*Bioprinters, resource roundabouts and braininternet? How we produce, consume and redistribute in 2050*]. Stichting Toekomstbeeld der Techniek, Den Haag.

Healy, J., D. Nicholson & P. Gahan (2017), *The future of work in Australia: Anticipating how new technologies will reshape labour markets, occupations and skill requirements.* Future Frontiers Analytical Report, NSW Department of Education, State of New South Wales.

Heijink, M. (2021), 'Windhandel of slimme investering?', *NRC*, zaterdag 13 maart & zondag 14 maart, p. 17.

Hessel, V. (2014), 'Megatrends—megascience?'. In: *Green Processing and Synthesis*, Vol. 3 Issue 2, pp. 99–100.

Hines, A. (2011), 'A dozen surprises about the future of work'. In: *Employment Relations Today*, Vol. 38 Issue 1, pp. 1–15.

Hishan, S.S., S. Ramakrishnan, M.I. Qureshi, N. Khan & N.H.S. Al-Kumaim (2020), 'Pandemic thoughts, civil infrastructure and sustainable development: Five insights from COVID-19 across travel lenses'. In: *Talent Development & Excellence*, Vol. 12 Issue 2, pp. 1690–1696.

Hofman, F. (2021), 'Robotisering zorgt juist voor méér banen [Robotization creates *more* jobs]'. In: *NRC*, 26 February, p. E9.

Hoppe, M., A. Christ, A. Castro, M. Winter & T.M. Seppanen (2014), 'Transformation in transportation?'. In: *European Journal of Futures Research*, Vol. 2 Issue 1, pp. 1–14.

Howcroft, D. & B. Bergvall-Kåreborn (2019), 'A typology of crowdwork platforms'. In: *Work, Employment and Society*, Vol. 33 Issue 1, pp. 21–38.

Hueck, H. (2021), 'Denemarken: coronapaspoort om naar kantoor te kunnen [Denmark: corona passport to be able to go to the office]'. In: *Het Financieele Dagblad*, 17 February.

Hughes, P., R.E. Morgan, I.R. Hodgkinson, Y. Kouropalatisb & A. Lindgreen (2020), 'A diagnostic tool to determine a strategic improvisation readiness index score (IRIS) to survive, adapt, and thrive in a crisis'. In: *Industrial Marketing Management*, Vol. 88, pp. 485–499.

Hyder, S. (2014), *7 things you can do to build an awesome personal brand*: www.forbes.com/sites/shamahyder/2014/08/18/7-things-you-can-do-to-build-an-awesome-personal-brand/#317a76683c3a.

Illanes, P., S. Lund, M. Mourshed, S. Rutherford & M. Tyreman (2018), *Retraining and reskilling workers in the age of automation*. McKinsey Global Institute, New York.

ILO (2017), *A study on the future of work in the Pacific*. ILO Office for Pacific Island Countries, International Labour Organization, Geneva.

Ingram, P. (2021), 'The forgotten dimension of diversity'. In: *Harvard Business Review*, Vol. 99 Issue 1, pp. 58–67.

IPCC (2021), *Climate change widespread, rapid, and intensifying*. Press release (August 9) based on the report Climate change 2021: The Physical Science Basis. Contribution of Working Group I to the Sixth Assessment Report of the Intergovernmental Panel on Climate Change, Geneva.

Jacobides, M.G. & M. Reeves (2020), 'Adapt your business to the new reality'. In: *Harvard Business Review*, Vol. 98 Issue 5, pp. 74–81.

Jayne, T. S., K. Yeboah & C. Henry (2017), *The future of work in African agriculture trends and drivers of change*. Report No. 994987492102676. Geneva: International Labour Organization.

Jonge, J. de & M.C. Peeters (2019), 'The vital worker: Towards sustainable performance at work'. In: *International Journal of Environmental Research and Public Health*, Vol. 16 Issue 6, p. 910.

Kaivo-Oja, J., S. Roth & L. Westerlund (2017), 'Futures of robotics: Human work in digital transformation'. In: *International Journal of Technology Management*, Vol. 73 Issue 4, pp. 176–205.

Kalse, E. (2021a), 'Vermogens rijksten weer terug op oude niveau [Wealth of richest people back to their old level]'. In: *NRC*, 25 January, p. 11.

Kalse, E. (2021b), 'Investeerder gaat MKB aan hogere klimaateisen houden [Investor will keep SMEs to higher climate requirements]'. In: *NRC*, 21 January, p. E5.

Kaplan, R.S., G. Serafeim & E. Tugendhat (2018), 'Inclusive growth: Profitable strategies for tackling poverty and inequality'. In: *Harvard Business Review*, Vol. 96 Issue 1, pp. 126–133.

Karabag, S.F. (2020), 'An unprecedented global crisis! The global, regional, national, political, economic and commercial impact of the coronavirus pandemic'. In: *Journal of Applied Economics & Business Research*, Vol. 10 Issue 1, pp. 1–6.

Kas, A. (2021), 'Vaker en vaker stroomt het zeewater Tasmins huis in [More and more often the seawater flows into Tasmin's house]'. In: *NRC*, 26 January, p. 15.

Kasriel, S. & C.E.O. Upwork (2018), 'The future of work won't be about college degrees, it will be about job skills'. *CNBC*: www.cnbc.com.

Kavanagh, M.M., H. Thirumurthy, R. Katz, K.L. Ebi, C. Beyrer, J. Headley, C.B. Holmes, C. Collins & L.O. Gostin (2019/2020), 'Ending pandemics: U.S. foreign policy to mitigate today's major killers, tomorrow's outbreaks, and the health impacts of climate change'. In: *Journal of International Affairs*, Vol. 73 Issue 1, pp. 49–68.

Kiel, D., J.M. Müller, C. Arnold & K.I. Voigt (2017), 'Sustainable industrial value creation: Benefits and challenges of industry 4.0'. In: *International Journal of Innovation Management*, Vol. 21 Issue 8, p. 1740015.

Kiss, M. (2017), *The future of work in the EU: Inventory of what various committees are planning to work on*. European Commission, Brussels.

Kniffin, K.M., J. Narayanan, F. Anseel, J. Antonakis, S.P. Ashford, A.B. Bakker, P. Bamberger, H. Bapuji, D.P. Bhave, V.K. Choi, S.J. Creary, E. Demerouti, F.J. Flynn, M.J. Gelfand, L.L. Greer, G. Johns, S. Kesebir, P.G. Klein, & Ozcelik H. Sun Young Lee (2020), 'COVID-19 in the workplace: Implications, issues, and insights for future research and action'. In: *American Psychologist*, Vol. 76 Issue 1, pp. 63–77.

Kochan, T.A. (2019), 'Shaping the future of work: Challenges and opportunities for U.S. labor management relations and workplace dispute resolution'. In: *Dispute Resolution Journal*, Vol. 74 Issue 1, pp. 11–31.

Kohlbacher, F. (2017), *Skills 4.0. How CEOs shape the future of work in Asia*. Center for Management Practice, Singapore Management University, Singapore.

Koonin, L.M. (2020), 'Novel coronavirus disease (COVID-19) outbreak: Now is the time to refresh pandemic plans'. In: *Journal of Business Continuity & Emergency Planning*, Vol. 13 Issue 4, pp. 298–312.

Kubicek, B. & C. Korunka (2017), 'The present and future of work: Some concluding remarks and reflections on upcoming trends'. In: C. Korunka & B. Kubicek (eds.), *Job demands in a changing world of work*. Springer, Cambridge, pp. 153–162.

Lamb, C. & S. Doyle (2017), *Future-proof: Preparing young Canadians for the future of work*. Brookfield Institute for Innovation Entrepreneurship, Toronto.

Lange, A.H. de (2019), *Succesvol ouder worden op het werk* [*Successful aging at work*]. Inaugural address, Open Universiteit, Heerlen.

Larson, R.C. & K.R. Nigmatulina (2010), 'Engineering responses to pandemics'. In: *Information Knowledge Systems Management*, Vol. 8 Issue 1–4, pp. 311–339.

Leijten, J. & M. Tamminga (2021), 'Poen, groen en de pandemie [Money, nature and the pandemic]'. In: *NRC*, 19 January, pp. E6–E7.

Lent, R.W. (2018), 'Future of work in the digital world: Preparing for instability and opportunity'. In: *The Career Development Quarterly*, Vol. 66 Issue 3, pp. 205–219.

Linthorst, J. & A. de Waal (2020), 'Disruptive forces and their postulated impact on organizations'. In: *Sustainability*, Vol. 12 Issue 20, paper 8740.

Livingston, R. (2020), 'How to promote racial equity in the workplace'. In: *Harvard Business Review*, Vol. 98 Issue 5, pp. 64–72.

Lund, S., J. Manyika & L.H. Segel (2019), *The future of work in America: People and places, today and tomorrow*. McKinsey Global Institute, New York.

Luttikhuis, P. (2021), 'Natuur heeft groot economisch belang [Nature has great economic importance]'. In: *NRC*, 12 March, p. 16.

MacEachen, E. (ed.) (2018), *The science and politics of work disability prevention*. Routledge, London.

Macomber, J.D. (2013), 'Building sustainable cities'. In: *Harvard Business Review*, Vol. 91 Issue 7–8, pp. 40–50.

Malik, R. & A.A. Janowska (2018), 'Megatrends and their use in economic analyses of contemporary challenges in the world economy'. In: *Research Papers of the Wroclaw University of Economics*, Issue 523, pp. 209–220.

Manpower Group (2020), *Closing the skills gap: What workers want*. Manpower Group: www.manpowergroup.ca.

Mansharamani, V. (2020), 'Harvard lecturer: "No specific skill will get you ahead in the future but this way of thinking will"'. *CNBC.com*: www.cnbc.com/2020/06/15/harvard-yale-researcher-future-success-is-not-a-specific-skill-its-a-type-of-thinking.html.

Manyika, J., M. Chui, A. Madgavkar & S. Lund (2017), *Technology, jobs, and the future of work*. McKinsey Global Institute, New York.

McGregor, S.L.T (2012), 'Bringing a life-centric perspective to influential megatrends'. In: D. Pendergast, S.L.T. McGregor & K. Turkki (eds.), *The next 100 years: Creating home economics futures*. Australian Academic Press, Queensland, pp. 24–37.

McMenamin, J.P. (2009), 'Pandemic influenza: Is there a corporate duty to prepare'. In: *Food & Drug LJ*, Vol. 64 Issue 1, pp. 69–100.

McQuay, L. (2018), 'Will robots duplicate or surpass us? The impact of job automation on tasks, productivity, and work'. In: *Psychosociological Issues in Human Resource Management*, Vol. 6 Issue 2, pp. 86–91.

Melaku, T.M., A. Beeman, D.G. Smith & W.B. Johnson (2020), 'Be a better ally'. In: *Harvard Business Review*, Vol. 98 Issue 6, pp. 135–139.

Menkveld, N. (2016), *Stedelijke distributie—thema update [Urban distribution—theme update]*. Economisch Bureau, Amsterdam, Nederland.

Menkveld, N. (2019), 'Stadslogistiek: Meer dan alleen pakketten [City logistics: More than just parcels]'. *Executive Finance*: https://executivefinance.nl/2016/12/stadslogistiek-meer-dan-alleen-pakketten/.

Merriman, K.K., S. Sen, A.J. Felo & B.E. Litzky (2016), 'Employees and sustainability: The role of incentives'. In: *Journal of Managerial Psychology*, Vol. 31 Issue 4, pp. 820–836.

Mittelstaedt, J.D., C.J. Shultz, W.E. Kilbourne & M. Peterson (2014), 'Sustainability as megatrend: Two schools of macromarketing thought'. In: *Journal of Macromarketing*, Vol. 34 Issue 3, pp. 253–264.

Mlambo, V.H. (2018), 'Cross-border migration in the Southern African development community (SADC): Benefits, problems and future prospects'. In: *Journal of Social and Development Sciences*, Vol. 8 Issue 4, pp. 42–56.

Morgan, J. (2020), *The Future Leader. 9 skills and mindsets to succeed in the next decade*. John Wiley & Sons, Hoboken.

Naisbitt, J. (1982), *Megatrends: Ten new directions transforming our lives.* Warner Books, New York.

Naisbitt, J. & P. Aburdene (1990), *Megatrends 2000: Ten new directions for the 1990's.* Morrow, New York.

National Intelligence Council (2012), *Global trends 2030: Alternative worlds.* National Intelligence Council: www.dni.gov/nic/globaltrends.

Noort, W. van (2021), 'De tirannie van de korte termijn [The tyranny of the short term]'. In: *NRC*, 20 January, p. C18.

Nooyi, I.K. & V. Govindarajan (2020), 'Becoming a better corporate citizen'. In: *Harvard Business Review*, Vol. 98 Issue 2, pp. 94–103.

Peciak R. (2016), 'Megatrends and their implications in the globalized world'. In: *Horyzonty Polityki*, Vol. 7, pp. 167–184.

Peetz, D. (2019), *The realities and futures of work.* Australian National University Press, Acton.

Pelgrim, C. & B. Rijlaarsdam (2021), 'Iedereen een vaste baan? Dat is niet de oplossing [Everybody a steady job? That's not the solution]'. In: *NRC*, 10 February, pp. E4–E5.

Piersma, J. (2021), 'Rechter wijst beroep op privacywetgeving af in conflict over GPS-horloges [Judge dismisses appeal to privacy legislation in conflict over GPS watches]'. In: *Het Financieele Dagblad*, 16 February, p. 23.

Pompa, C. (2015), *Jobs for the future.* Overseas Development Institute, London.

PWC (2019), *The road to circularity: Why a circular economy is becoming the new normal.* PricewaterhouseCoopers B.V., Amsterdam.

Ransome, P. (2019), *Sociology and the future of work: Contemporary discourses and debates.* Routledge, London.

Ratanjee, V. (2020), *4 ways to continue employee development when budgets are cut.* Gallup, Washington, DC.

Ray, K. & T.A. Thomas (2019), 'Online outsourcing and the future of work'. In: *Journal of Global Responsibility*, Vol. 10 Issue 3, pp. 226–238.

Retief, F., A. Bond, J. Pope, A. Morrison-Saunders & N. King (2016), 'Global megatrends and their implications for environmental assessment practice'. In: *Environmental Impact Assessment Review*, Vol. 61, pp. 52–60.

Rohrbeck, R., M.E. Kum, T. Jissink & A.W. Gordon (2018), *Corporate foresight benchmarking report 2018: How leading firms build a superior position in markets of the future.* Aarhus Universiteit School of Business and Social Sciences, Aarhus.

Rudolph, C.W., J. Marcus, R. Mah & H. Zacher (2018), 'Global issues in work, aging, and retirement'. In: K.S. Shultz & G.A. Adams (eds.), *Aging and work in the 21st century.* Taylor & Francis Inc., London, pp. 292–324.

Sanchez-Reaza, J., G. Alves & L. Berniell (2018), *The future of work.* Urban 20 White Paper, Urban20: www.urban20.org.

Shankar, K. (2020), 'The impact of COVID-19 on IT services industry—expected transformations'. In: *British Journal of Management*, Vol. 31 Issue 3, pp. 450–452.

Shih, W.C. (2020), 'Global supply chains in a post-pandemic world: Companies need to make their networks more resilience. Here is how'. In: *Harvard Business Review*, September–October, pp. 83–89.

SHRM (2020), *COVID-19 Research: How the pandemic is challenging and changing employers.* SHRM research report: https://shrm.org/hr-today/trends-and-forecasting/research-and-surveys/Pages/.

Sloan Center on Aging & Work (2012), *CVS caremark snowbird program.* Boston College, Boston.

Smet, A. de, C. Gagnon & E. Mygatt (2021), *Organizing for the future. Nine keys to becoming a future-ready company.* McKinsey & Company, Chicago.

Smith, P.A.C. & C. Sharicz (2011), 'The shift needed for sustainability'. In: *The Learning Organization*, Vol. 18 Issue 1, pp. 73–86.

Smith, S. (2020), *How to future: Leading and sense-making in an age of hyperchange.* Kogan Page, London.

Sondermeijer, V. (2021), 'Bouwen met hout? De norm helpt beton [Building with wood? The standard helps concrete]'. In: *NRC*, 21 January, p. E4.

Straaten, F. van (2021), 'Bereid je voor op een slinkende en grijzere wereldbevolking [Prepare for a dwindling and grayer world population]'. In: *NRC*, 2 February, pp. 14–15.

Thoroughgood, C.N., K.B. Sawyer & J.R. Webster (2020), 'Creating a trans-inclusive workplace'. In: *Harvard Business Review*, Vol. 98 Issue 2, pp. 114–123.

Tinnilä, M. (2012), 'Impact of future trends on banking services'. In: *Journal of Internet Banking and Commerce*, Vol. 17 Issue 2, pp. 1–15.

Toe Laer, E. (2021), 'Nieuwkomer zoekt werk—Ja, ook tijdens lastige coronacrisis [Newcomer is looking for work—yes, even during a difficult corona crisis]'. In: *Het Financieele Dagblad*, 5 January, pp. 10–11.

Torres, N. (2018), 'Are there good jobs in the gig economy?'. In: *Harvard Business Review*, Vol. 96 Issue 4, pp. 146–14.

United Nations (2019a), *World population prospects 2019.* Department of Economic and Social Affairs, United Nations, New York.

United Nations (2019b), *Global issues/climate change*: www.un.org/en/sections/issues-depth/climate-change/index.html.

Verbeke, A. (2020), 'Will the COVID-19 pandemic really change the governance of global value chains?'. In: *British Journal of Management*, Vol. 31 Issue 3, pp. 444–446.

VNO-NCW en MKB-Nederland (2019), *Afrika Strategie Nederlands bedrijfsleven [Africa strategy Dutch businesses].* VNO-NCW en MKB-Nederland, Den Haag.

Von der Gracht, H.A. & I.L. Darkow (2010), 'The future role of logistics for global wealth—scenarios and discontinuities until 2025'. In: *Foresight*, Vol. 15 Issue 5, pp. 405–419.

Waal, A.A. de (2012), *What makes a high performance organization: Five validated factors of competitive performance that apply worldwide.* Global Professional Publishing, Enfield.

Waal, A.A. de (2013), 'Evergreens of excellence'. In: *Journal of Management History*, Vol. 19 Issue 2, pp. 241–278.

Waal, A.A. de & H. de Wit (2018), 'Managers zijn tevredener dan medewerkers: hoe erg is het?', *Tijdschrift voor Ontwikkeling in Organisaties*, no. 1.

Waal, A.A. de (2020), *High-performance managerial leadership, best ideas from around the world*. Praeger, Santa Barbara.

Waal, A.A. de (2021), 'The high performance organization: Proposed definition and measurement of its performance'. In: *Measuring Business Excellence*, Vol. 25.

Waal, A.A. de & R. Goedegebuure (2017), 'Investigating the causal link between a management improvement technique and organizational performance: The case of the HPO framework'. In: *Management Research Review*, Vol. 40 Issue 4, pp. 429–450.

Waal, A.A. de & J. Linthorst (2020), 'Future-proofing the high-performing organization'. In: *Sustainability*, Vol. 12 Issue 12, paper 8507.

Waal, A. de, J. Linthorst & C. Hetterschijt (2021), 'Lessons learned by Organizations during the COVID-19 pandemic'. In: *International Journal of Management and Applied Research*, Vol. 8 Issue 1, pp. 72–90.

Waal, A. de, L. Peters & M. Broekhuizen (2017), 'Do different generations look differently at high performance organizations?'. In: *Journal of Strategy and Management*, Vol. 10 Issue 1, pp. 86–101.

Wagenaar, K. (2020), *Business unusual*. Boom Uitgevers, Amsterdam.

Walle, E. van der (2021), 'Grote beleggers hekelen klimaatbeleid bedrijven [Major investors criticize companies' climate policy]'. In: *NRC*, 23 March, p. E2.

Wang, Y., A. Hong, X. Li, & J. Gao (2020), 'Marketing innovations during a global crisis: A study of China firms' response to COVID-19'. In: *Journal of Business Research*, Vol. 116, pp. 214–220.

Whelan, T. & E. Douglas (2021), 'How to talk to your CFO about sustainability'. In: *Harvard Business Review*, Vol. 99 Issue 1, pp. 86–93.

Whiteley, G. & J. Casasbuenas (2020), *Partnerships for skills: Learning from digital frontrunner countries*. Nesta, London.

Wiel, C. van de (2021), 'Deglobalisering is een illusie [Deglobalization is an illusion]'. In: *NRC*, 23 March, p. E5.

Wienen, J. (2021), 'Geen brief, meteen aan de slag [No letter, get started right away]'. In: *NRC*, 25 March, p. E7.

Williams, J.C. & S. Mihaylo (2019), 'How the best bosses interrupt bias on their teams'. In: *Harvard Business Review*, Vol. 97 Issue 6, pp. 151–155.

Winkel, R. (2021), 'FNV boekt overwinning in de strijd tegen schijnzelfstandigheid [FNV wins in the fight against bogus self-employment]'. In: *Het Financieele Dagblad*, 17 February, p. 5.

Woetzel, J., A. Madgavkar, R. Khaled, F. Mattern, J. Bughin, J. Manyika & A. Hasyagar (2016), *People on the move. Global migration's impact and opportunity*. McKinsey Global Institute, New York.

World Bank (2019), *World development report 2019: The changing nature of wrk*. World Bank, Washington, DC.

World Economic Forum (2018a), *The future of jobs report 2018*. World Economic Forum, Geneva, Switzerland.

World Economic Forum (2018b), *Eight futures of work scenarios and their implications*. Whitepaper in preparation of The Future of Work Project, World Economic Forum, Geneva, Switzerland.

Zahidi, S., V. Ratcheva, G. Hingel & S. Brown (2020), *The future of jobs report 2020*. World Economic Forum, Geneva.

Zbierowski, P. (2020), 'The mystery of high performance—mediation by entrepreneurial orientation and organizational citizenship behavior'. In: *Journal of Entrepreneurship, Management and Innovation*, Vol. 16 Issue 2, pp. 3–26.

Index

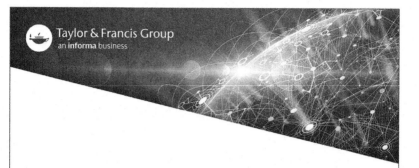

Printed in the United States
by Baker & Taylor Publisher Services